Lillian Too
Jennifer T

FORTU

2021

KONSEPBOOKS
ASTROLOGY . FENG SHUI . INSPIRATIONS

Fortune & Feng Shui 2021 Dog

by *Lillian Too* and *Jennifer Too*

Published by KONSEP LAGENDA SDN BHD (223 855)
Kuala Lumpur 59100 Malaysia

For more Konsep books, go to *www.lillian-too.com* or *www.wofs.com*
To report errors, please send a note to errors@konsepbooks.com
For general feedback, email feedback@konsepbooks.com

ISBN 978-967-2929-03-1
Published in Malaysia, September 2020

DOG 2021

BIRTH YEAR	WESTERN CALENDAR DATES	AGE	KUA NUMBER MALES	KUA NUMBER FEMALES
Wood Dog	14 Feb 1934 - 3 Feb 1935	87	3 East Group	3 East Group
Fire Dog	2 Feb 1946 - 21 Jan 1947	75	9 East Group	6 West Group
Earth Dog	18 Feb 1958 - 7 Feb 1959	63	6 West Group	9 East Group
Metal Dog	6 Feb 1970 - 26 Jan 1971	51	3 East Group	3 East Group
Water Dog	25 Jan 1982 - 12 Feb 1983	39	9 East Group	6 West Group
Wood Dog	10 Feb 1994 - 30 Jan 1995	27	6 West Group	9 East Group
Fire Dog	29 Jan 2006 - 17 Feb 2007	15	3 East Group	3 East Group

Introduction to the Year 2021

Chapter 1

YEAR OF THE METAL OX

The coming year is the Year of the Metal Ox, a year when harvests are reaped as a result of old-fashioned hard work. It takes on the nature of the diligent Ox, whose finest qualities are its stability and steadfastness, the sign that symbolizes all the hard work that has to be done in order to prepare for the harvests and prosperity that follows. While the coming year can be prolific, there are few shortcuts to be had. Those who put in the hours and who match their effort with their wit will be those who reap the most from the year. This will not be a time for easy money or overnight speculative gains. It will be a year when substance wins out over panache, and when those who put emphasis on building solid foundations will prosper. One should strive to work first at what one can bring to the table, before making promises or trying to convince others of one's potential.

THE TOILING OX

This is the year of the Metal Ox, so it is one in which the Earth element of the Ox gets constantly exhausted by its heavenly stem of Metal. Earth produces Metal, so is exhausted by it. This is a year when the Ox has to constantly keep up its efforts to stay ahead. Individuals who are dedicated and disciplined will be the most effective and the most successful. The year can be an powerful, and power here has to potential to corrupt. Checks and balances become more important, as the year could produce leaders who make unscrupulous decisions, taking into account only their own personal agendas.

This affliction affects not just leaders on the world stage but those in one's immediate sphere as well – bosses, community leaders, mentors, teachers, parents. If this Metal energy is not kept under control, it could lead to disastrous consequences in one's personal daily life. The effects of this can feel very real and close to home.

WHAT TO DO: We suggest displaying a **red-faced Kuan Kung**, the powerful Warrior God in the home and office to protect against the excess of Metal element energy. Having this God of War and God of Wealth in the home ensures you stay on the winning side of the element luck effect. Kuan Kung will ensure you make judicious decisions that end up benefiting you and your family in the long run. Gives you courage to move forward but tempers any misplaced bravado.

Red-faced Kuan Kung with 5 victory flags

2. Wearing jewellery in precious Metals fashioned as **sacred syllables** and **symbols** transforms the effect of Metal from autocratic to benevolent. It helps keep you protected from harm and ensures you do not lose the support of the people who matter most to your prospects in life- eg. Your boss, your parents, your teachers.

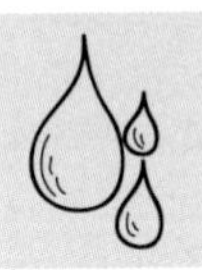

WATER *represents competition*

WATER in 2021 stands for FRIENDS and FOES, which are present in equal measure. Both have an equivalent part to play in the outcomes that follow. Because the year is one of STRONG WATER, the element of Water this year needs to be treated with caution. Too much of it could tip the scales over, attracting fierce rivalry and underhand tactics by one's competition, rather than cultivating strong allies that stay loyal.

This year it becomes especially important to carry protective amulets that guard against betrayal and disloyalty. Carrying an image of **Kuan Kung with Anti-Betrayal Amulet** will help protect against becoming a victim of these energies. Always give others suitable respect, and don't disregard the dangers of allies changing sides. If the incentive becomes attractive enough, they will. Don't take anything too personally if you can adopt the stoic outlook of the Ox where you make the most of the opportunities open to you without complaining too much what is fair or not fair. You can effectively buffer against many of the pitfalls of the year.

THE COLOR BLUE – Blacks and blues stand for Water energy. While water to the Chinese traditionally represents money, this year it also signifies competition. Using too much of this color this year holds the danger of fueling rivalry and competitiveness amongst one's peers. Do not don too much black, and when you do, try to add a splash of color to neutralize its more sinister effects. Place the **Celestial Water Dragon** in the home to keep this element under control.

FIRE *brings wealth*

FIRE in 2021 stands for WEALTH LUCK. This is the element that appears to be completely missing from the year's chart and thus is the one we must actively work at replacing. There is hidden wealth brought by the Tiger, but this needs a trigger for it to be actualized. We suggest wearing the color red in free abandon this year. Remember, this is the Year of the Ox, an Earth sign whose inner vitality gets spurred on by the wonderful energy of Fire.

THE COLOR RED - Red to the Chinese is always considered lucky. It is a color of celebration and carnival. It is traditionally used in all auspicious occasions, and as we move into the new year of 2021, it is especially important to wear plenty of red! For the first 15 days of the Lunar New Year, we recommend getting yourself a red outfit for each day. Keep up this ritual through the entire 15 days of celebrations to ensure its effects can get you through the year. This is an excellent way to "fuel up" for the year, as it is a year when the element of Fire is glaringly missing.

In the home, keep the lights bright throughout the year. Change your lightbulbs whenever they start to flicker or lose energy, and don't try to save on the electricity bill by constantly turning off the lights! It is far more important to work at keeping this element properly energized through the year. Don't be penny wise and pound foolish. Lights represent Fire energy, and Fire energy represents wealth and prosperity in 2021.

NEW WEALTH WALLET: Each year it is an extremely lucky ritual to get yourself a new wallet and transfer some money from your old wallet over to your new one, while adding in some brand new notes (best if from cash received as a Chinese New Year ang pow, or from one's latest drawn salary or bonus). You can also keep an image of the **Wealth God Sitting on**

a Tiger in the form of a Gold Card inside your wallet; very auspicious as the Tiger is the sign that brings hidden wealth to the year.

Each year we design a wallet to vibrate and sync with the energies of the year, and for 2021, our wealth wallet features the stock market bull. It is the Year of the Ox and the Wall Street Bull is a most auspicious symbolic cousin of the sign of the year. The Wall Street Bull represents your investments going up, and your asset wealth growing.

We also have the **Asset Wealth Bull with Wealth Amulet** which will attract wealth-generating luck to any home which invites it in. Display prominently in the West where the *Star of Current Prosperity* has flown to this year or on your desk in front of you where you work. The idea is to see it daily and its subliminal effects will magically influence your actions and ability to attract wealth luck into your life.

WOOD *brings growth*

WOOD is the element that stands for growth. In 2021, it also signifies intelligence and creativity. It is what brings fresh new ideas to the mix, encouraging a blossoming of imagination and ingenuity. As we foray further into the new decade, old ideas will increasingly lose appeal and old technologies become obsolete with increasing speed. These need to be replaced and they will, and it will be those who can dream up the new ideas, methods, designs and technologies that will profit.

For the individual looking at making it in a rapidly changing world, it will be enhanced creativity and thinking outside the box that will help you. Surround yourself with the vibrant energy of plants and greenery, invite fresh flowers displayed in auspicious vases into your living space. If you live in a modern skyscraper city where feasting on green is difficult or unusual, look for ways to introduce indoor gardens into your home and office space, take regular time to visit parks and gardens, or make time to visit the countryside to refuel and recharge your senses with the power of nature.

THE COLOR GREEN – Greens of all kinds represent innovation and vision in 2021. Fill your wardrobe with lots of this color in emerald green, lime green, neon green, shamrock, chartreuse, sage, seafoam… all of these will inject your wardrobe with a fresh dash of inspiration and will attract wonderfully inspired energies into your aura. Green this year is very lucky and brings to the wearer a new lease of life. If you have been feeling dull, uninspired or at a crossroads, introducing a pop of bright green into what you wear or carry will give you the boost you need to change track, get moving, get started. It is the "energizing" colour of the year and should be made use of liberally and profusely.

TEND TO YOUR GARDEN: There's nothing that invokes better yang Wood energy than thriving plants and greenery. Make a trip to your local nursery and bring home some vibrant new plants to add to your garden. If you live in an apartment, introduce some live potted plants into your living space. This will stir up the creative juices in you needed to dream up new ideas and to hatch ingenious strategies for your work and in your life.

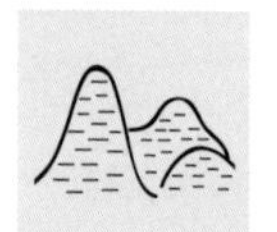

EARTH *brings power & influence*

EARTH in the Year of the Ox is the intrinsic element of the animal sign of the year. It is the element that symbolizes stability, strength and permanence. It is the element that ensures that however crazy the energy gets, however quickly the world changes around us, we can dig our heels deep and stay grounded with our values and our visions intact. Earth energy will prevent us being light-eared and light-headed, or easily influenced. In 2021, the element of EARTH also signifies recognition and power. It brings the luck of rank and position, and boosts one's chances when it comes to promotion and upward mobility, whether in one's career or in any climb to the top of any organization. Earth energy brings you influence and command and will make people listen to you.

EARTH COLORS – Wearing shades of earth tones brings you respect and makes people listen to you. It keeps you rational and well-balanced and envelops you with an aura of dependability. An excellent color group to use when you need others to take you seriously. Earth colors include yellow, orange, beige and cream, in all their shades. Wear such colors when you feel you need others to take notice of you, when you want to boost your influence over others and when you need people to listen to you. Those of you ambitious for your career to get a boost will benefit greatly from making use of earth colors.

THE 24 MOUNTAINS CHART OF 2021

The compass wheel around which the animals are positioned contain 24 mountains which attract different stars each year. The overall fortunes of the year get enhanced or disabled depending on which stars settle into which corners. Some years will have

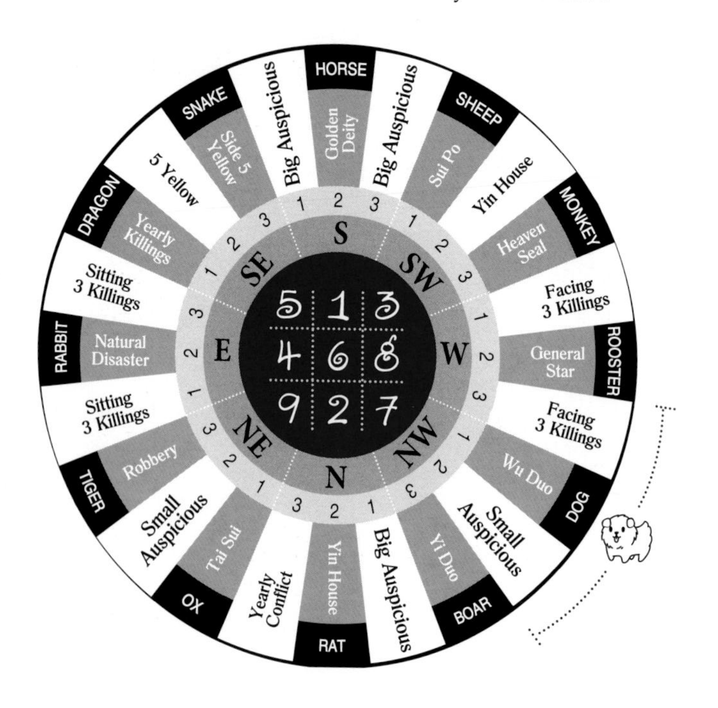

more auspicious stars, and some less, and their positions around the wheel impact on each animal sign differently.

THE LUCK OF BIG & SMALL AUSPICIOUS

One of the luckiest indications from this chart are the Big and Small Auspicious Stars, and in 2021, we have 5 of such stars making an appearance. The year enjoys three *Big Auspicious* stars and two *Small Auspicious* stars. The animal signs that benefit from these are the **Horse**, **Snake**, **Sheep**, **Rat**, **Boar**, the **Dog**, **Ox** and **Tiger**. The locations of these stars are spread out giving the above animal signs the potential to seize opportunities that come their way.

The sign that benefits most from this indication is the **HORSE**. The Horse enjoys two Big Auspicious stars, which suggests that after two difficult years, this sign is ready to take flight. The free-spirited Horse person can finally seize what it has been grappling after; this is a year when this sign can take risks and put wholehearted effort behind their passions. It is a year when the Horse should not rest on its laurels, because the big time has arrived.

The other signs enjoying Big Auspicious are the **Snake** and **Sheep**, and the **Rat** and **Boar**. These signs also have the potential to go after big dreams and, to realize big ambitions they may have been harboring.

For these signs, opportunities will be plentiful. Success comes for those who are hungry and resolute. Remember that this year, results do not come immediately, so one must not get discouraged if the path to actualization seems long or even impossible. The winners will be those with the staying power to keep at it and stay the course. Hold on to your dreams, and don't change your mind at every setback. Trust in your instincts and passions, and don't give power to those who disturb your mind or pour cold water on your ideas.

While the Stars of Big Auspicious bring really fabulous blessings, so do the Stars of Small Auspicious. These have the same effect as their big brother stars, but they bring success in smaller measures and in stages. The signs enjoying Small Auspicious this year are the **Ox**, **Tiger**, **Dog** and **Boar.** For these signs, they are likely to meet with small successes that form the stepping stones to bigger success later on. For these signs, this is a year for building firm foundations and laying out the pathway for future triumphs.

Small Auspicious brings end goals that hold slightly longer time trajectories, but accompanied with the same staying power, success does ultimately come. Learn to celebrate the smallest of wins and stay clearheaded about your ultimate goals. If you constantly step back to examine the bigger picture, you will not lose sight of why you are doing what you're doing.

ENHANCER: Remember that *Stars of Big and Small Auspicious* bring the potential of great fortune, but to enjoy their benefits to the fullest, they need to be enhanced. Each year then, we design a Big Auspicious Enhancer to kickstart the very positive effects of these stars. This year, all animal signs benefit from displaying the **Six Birds Auspicious Multiplier**. This activator featuring an I-Ching coin with six birds and the auspicious amulet enhancer brings new opportunities. The 6 birds activates the #6 Heaven Star that rules the year's Lo Shu chart. The number 6 is the number of the heavens, which unlocks the celestial hand of the Gods. Display this potent activator in a place where you can see it often – either in a prominent place in the home, or in front of you on your work desk.

6 Birds Auspicious Multiplier. Unlocks the Big Auspicious luck of the year.

LUCK FROM THE HEAVENS

Two stars that further magnify the luck of the heavens are the *Golden Deity Star* and the *Star of the Heavenly Seal*. These land in the location of the **Horse** and the **Monkey**, bringing these two signs the luck of celestial fortunes. For these two signs, help comes without having to seek it. They enjoy the patronage of powerful mentors with many wishing to help them. They also have better instincts and can trust their own judgment more. For the Horse, as it also enjoys two Big Auspicious stars, little can go wrong as long as it stays judicious and diligent. The Monkey however needs to employ its trademark cunning to make the most of the Heaven Seal; it has to dodge the Yin House and Facing 3 Killings, but its main 24 Mountain star influence is extremely positive.

To make the most of these stars, we recommend that the Horse and Monkey invite in a **Golden Deity** into the home. Any Buddha, God or holy figure in line with your own faith will work. We particularly love **Kuan Yin, the Goddess of Mercy**, revered by Chinese all around the world. She is the female personification of the compassionate Buddha and brings wealth, health and happiness and protection from harm.

Kuan Yin

THE GENERAL STAR

The **Rooster** enjoys the General Star, which brings it power and authority, but unfortunately also fuels its short fuse and hot temper. But the Rooster this year has the very lucky #8 star, which enhances its fortunes and intrinsic energy. The Rooster as a sign does not suffer fool's gladly, so all these indications point to a Rooster that reigns supreme in 2021, but one who may be insufferable to those it considers "beneath" them, whether in intelligence or in status. To make the most of this star, all Roosters this year benefit from displaying the **Power Ru Yi**, the scepter of authority which boosts its command as boss or leader, while ensuring no disgruntled subordinates try to make trouble, or rivals rise up to try to displace it.

Star of the Yin House

This star brings danger of sickness and disease, and a general lack of energy to those it afflicts. It is particularly dangerous if one is already ill or elderly, or with other heavy afflictions indicated in their charts. This year, there are two Yin House stars and these arrive in the SW and North, affecting the **Sheep**, **Monkey** and **Rat**. All three of these signs are advised to take more care this year when it comes to health, well-being and safety. We strongly suggest that these signs carry protective amulets to shield them from the influence of malevolent spirits that may wreak havoc in their lives. Any of the **seed syllables Om, Ah or**

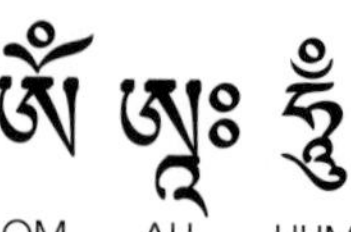

Hum will invoke the presence of the mighty Buddha, establishing a firm spiritual circumference of protection around the wearer.

If ill health is of particular concern, we recommend wearing and displaying health amulets. The **Wu Lou**, **Garuda Bird**, and the **Healing Deer**, bring precious cosmic protection. The deer is especially wonderful; this animal has always been associated with health, strength and vigor. It is also the animal that holds the solution to good health when all other methods have not seemed to work. There are many folk legends associated with the deer in all cultures, but in Chinese mythology, the deer is almost always shown accompanying Sau, the divine God of Longevity.

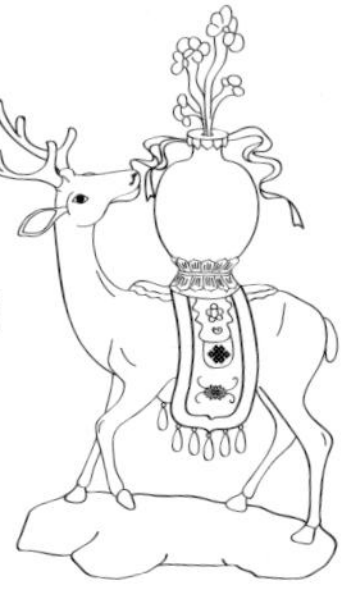

Healing Deer

The Robbery Star

This star brings money loss and betrayal and especially affects the **Tiger** in 2021. Those born under this sign need to be especially mindful not to get taken in by con men and getting cheated by others. There is higher chance of getting conned into undertaking bad investments. Business partners and associates could prove untrustworthy. It is also very important whenever one has this affliction to take care of personal safety. Robberies, muggings, petty thieves and street crime become more of a danger. This star also brings risk of becoming a victim of chance or collateral damage in somebody else's fight.

To counter this negative star, you need the image of the **Blue Rhino and Elephant** in the home, and you MUST carry the **Anti Robbery Amulet**. This protects against losing money and possessions. It is also important to protect against personal harm and injury; wear protective amulet at all times! Females in particular should avoid venturing out alone late at night or putting themselves under unnecessary risk; they should carry the **Nightspot Protection Amulet** for protection against petty crime.

Anti Robbery Amulet

Yearly Conflict & Yearly Killings

These stars bring obstacles to everything you do, making it difficult to make meaningful progress. These are the stars that can discourage you from remaining steadfast and keeping on your intended path. It throws up unexpected snags and hitches, and when left unchecked, can overwhelm one with feelings of depression and anxiety. These are negative stars that gather the slings and arrows of misfortune hurling them your way with some measure of ferocity. It is as such extremely important to take note of their location each year and take definite steps to neutralize them.

In 2021, the Yearly Killings star has landed in the **Dragon**'s location of SE1, and the Yearly Conflict Star visits the N3 sector, affecting the animal signs of **Rat** and **Ox**.

The *Yearly Killings Star* is deadlier and needs immediate action – we suggest that all Dragon-born and all those whose bedrooms or main door location are in the SE carry the **28 Hums Protection Wheel** and invite in the **Buddha image of Nangsi Zilnon Guru Rinpoche**. He is the warrior Buddha who completely overcomes all types of obstacles brought by the Yearly Killings.

28 Hums Protection Wheel

The *Yearly Conflict Star* makes everyone want to fight with you, bringing opposition to your ideas and making it difficult to see your projects through. Working in teams becomes especially difficult. At work, this could mean difficult colleagues and fierce politicking by workplace rivals. Those afflicted by this star could find themselves spending the better part of their time dodging potshots rather than focusing on their work. It makes work life very unpleasant, and the effects of this star can also permeate one's social and private life. This negative star arrives in the N3 sector affecting all whose main door or bedroom or office are located in this part of the home or office, and it affects Rat and Ox born people. Those affected by this affliction need to carry protection amulets and display the relevant cures. The **Dorje Drolo Scorpion Amulet** is especially helpful in this regard.

Natural Disaster Star

This star arrives in the East sector, affecting those who spend much time in this part of the home. This is the star that puts in you in harm's way – being at the wrong place at the wrong time. It brings all manner of natural misfortune including floods, fires, earthquakes, tsunamis, viruses and disease. If you are afflicted by this star, you MUST carry spiritual protection. ALL East-facing homes benefit from inviting in a statue of **Guru Rinpoche**, and all living in homes facing East should wear the **Bhrum Pendant** which protects against all kinds of harm, illness, accidents and avoidable misfortune.

LUCK OF THE 12 ANIMAL SIGNS

Every animal sign is affected by a host of factors which change each year, producing a different basket of combinations which influence each individual sign's luck differently. Aside from the animal sign year you were born under, there are additional factors affecting your luck, but viewed together with these indications, anyone can alter the course of their lives and make intelligent decisions to maximize luck through any given year.

Here we summarize the broad outlook for the different animal signs, and in later chapters of this book, we go into greater depth and detail on what all of this means for you personally, depending on your heavenly stem, your home direction, your lunar mansion and your compatibilities.

The **HORSE** is blessed with extremely fortunate indications with the double *stars of Big Auspicious* and the *Star of Golden Deity* brought by the 24 Mountains Compass of 2021. This sign has great good fortune coming, which should more than make up for the unfortunate stars it had to endure in the last two years. The Horse is an energetic and restless sign full of passion and appetite for adventure, but the last couple of years will have made it difficult for it to pursue its desires. This year changes all of this; the Horse person will feel like a cloud has lifted, and as the year progresses, things get better and better. There are no unlucky indications at all, and the Victory Star #1 promises some very exciting new developments in the Horse's life.

The Horse should boost its fortunes with the **6 Birds Auspicious Multiplier** and benefits from displaying the **Desktop Flag of Victory** in its vicinity.

Desktop Flag of Victory

The **MONKEY** and **ROOSTER** are the signs enjoying the luckiest element luck indications. These two Metal signs have superlative Life Force and Spirit Essence, suggesting an inner determination that is unwavering. These signs know exactly what it is they want and how to go about getting it. Both Monkey and Rooster are known for their innate intelligence and ingenuity, and their already immense brainpower gets a big boost this year. The Monkey in particular enjoys very promising "success" luck; not only can it get what it wants, it receives plenty of recognition to go along with it too!

The **Rooster** can boost success luck by surrounding itself with the presence of the **Victorious Windhorse Carrying a Jewel**, as can the Monkey. Both these signs also have excellent indications from the 24 Mountains, with Monkey enjoying the *Heaven Seal* and Rooster benefitting from the *General Star*. The Monkey should carry the **Dragon Heavenly Seal Amulet** and the Rooster needs the **Ru Yi**.

The sign that gets hit by the *Five Yellow* this year are the **DRAGON** and **SNAKE**. This indicates that these signs need to watch that the *wu wang* does not bring misfortune their way. The Five Yellow of 2021 sits in a Wood sector, which suggests it is NOT a deadly Five Yellow; nevertheless, the obstacles it brings can cause life to feel very unpleasant indeed and it should be strongly subdued.

Dragon and Snake this year need to carry the **Five Element Pagoda Amulet with Tree of Life** to combat the afflictive energy, turning obstacles into productive challenges, and transforming unfortunate outcomes into promising ones. Both Dragon and Snake are signs that thrive in adversity, gaining strength and shrewdness when the going gets tough. And the *wu wang* of this year can be metamorphosed into positive rather than negative results. The Snake should have the **6 Birds Auspicious Multiplier**, while the Dragon needs the **28 Hums Protection Wheel**.

The WOOD ELEMENT SIGNS of **TIGER** and **RABBIT** both enjoy very good element indications but need to boost success luck with the **Victorious Windhorse** this year. The Tiger benefits from the *Small Auspicious*, and direct access to the hidden wealth of the year, but the Rabbit needs to do more work to boost its prosperity potential. The Tiger should display the **6 Birds Auspicious Multiplier** while the Rabbit MUST carry the **Three Celestial Shields Amulet** to stay protected against the 3 Killings affliction that affects it this year.

The WATER ELEMENT SIGNS of **RAT** and **BOAR** are the most unfortunate in terms of element luck, facing very bad life force and spirit essence. This can cause a sudden lack of confidence in one's own abilities and make these two signs prone to being easily discouraged. What the Rat and Boar need this year are strong cures to lift their inner energies. They need to carry the **Life Force Amulet** and **"Om" Dakini Spirit Enhancing Amulet**. What these two signs do have however are a shared *Big Auspicious Star*. Rat and Boar working together can produce very favourable results, and their affinity with each other gets enhanced this year. These two signs will make good business partners. Of the two, Rat will be luckier than Boar, and should take the lead in any endeavor they embark on together.

"Om" Dakini Spirit Enhancing Amulet

The EARTH SIGNS of **OX, DOG, DRAGON** and **SHEEP** all have good life force but bad spirit essence. This suggests that for these signs, they have decent inherent energy, but exposure to the wrong company could be harmful to their mindsets and their motivation levels. They are spiritually weaker than usual and need to carry the **"Om" Dakini Spirit Enhancing Amulet**. Those who are spiritual in nature can draw strength from their belief systems and find solace and comfort in their spiritual practice.

The **SHEEP** meanwhile is also in direct clash with the TAI SUI of the year, and hence the priority for this sign should be to take all steps to appease the God of the Year. The Sheep needs the **Tai Sui Amulet**, and its celestial guardian animal this year should be

Tai Sui Amulet

the **Dragon Pi Yao**. The Sheep can lean on its special friend the Horse, who enjoys superlative luck in 2021. The Sheep working or hanging out with a Horse in the coming year will benefit tremendously from its astrological soulmate. But all four Earth signs are in direct or indirect conflict with the Year God and should thus ALL carry the **Tai Sui Amulet** and have his plaque in the home.

WEALTH LUCK IN 2021

Wealth luck this coming year is weak. It will be difficult to make quick money. Wealth that gets created will come from hard work rather than speculative gains. The year continues to see much disruption to the way business is done, making things difficult for those in sunset industries. Individuals who can spot new opportunities can profit, but increasingly, the free flow of information will reduce the time window for monopolies in new industries. It will be creativity and originality, together with consistent hard work that will allow individuals and businesses to generate income in 2021.

As machines take over more and more jobs, those who do not do something and stubbornly hang on to an old way of life could quickly find themselves being made redundant. The year will not be an easy one for wealth creation, and macro level events continue to depress the immediate outlook.

Certain animal signs will have element luck in their favour when it comes to wealth luck this year; even so, the advice is to weigh all decisions carefully before making them. This is a year when one can take risks, but do not put all your eggs in one basket. Make sure any risks taken are calculated ones backed by understanding and research.

WEALTH ENHANCER: All individuals benefit from inviting in wealth enhancers, particularly the **Asset Wealth Bull** which boosts money and income luck, but also protects against your assets losing value. Those invested in the stock market would benefit greatly from the presence of this bull in the home. It has been designed to look like the stock market bull on Wall Street and carries the meaning "May the market bull for you"; it also features auspicious symbols of good fortune, a red saddle to represent prosperity in 2021, and it is shown presiding over a pile of coins and ingots, signifying its control and dominance over cash. With this bull, you will always have enough money, and even those who sustain losses will quickly make it back.

Asset Wealth Bull

GETTING YOUR TIMING RIGHT:
The Dog in 2021 benefits from carrying or having the **"White Tiger" Constellation Lucky Charms** near them this year. The Tiger Constellation of the Lunar Mansions features 7 Sky Animals that work in tandem to ensure you get your timing just right whenever you need to make important moves or decisions. These lucky charms bring out all of the Tiger's positive attributes. Remember, the Tiger is the sign who feeds the coming year with hidden wealth; it is also the astrological ally of the Dog. Its lunar constellation meanwhile includes the Sky Dog amongst its 7 Sky Animals.

"White Tiger" Constellation Lucky Charms

LOVE LUCK IN 2021

SINGLES CAN FIND LOVE IN 2021

For singles, this is a promising year for romance. The *Peach Blossom Star* has settled into the East, a WOOD sector, which gives it strength. The East is also the palace of the Rabbit, which is associated with the Moon and Moon Goddess who presides over fortunes related to love and romance. She bestows wishes to do with relationships, aids in matchmaking soulmates, and improves relations between married couples.

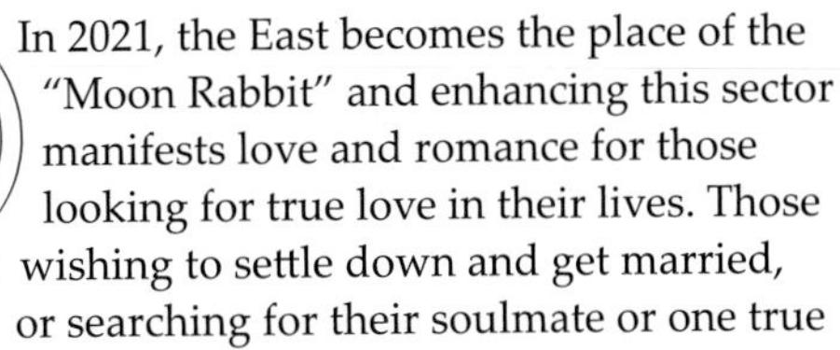

In 2021, the East becomes the place of the "Moon Rabbit" and enhancing this sector manifests love and romance for those looking for true love in their lives. Those wishing to settle down and get married, or searching for their soulmate or one true love, displaying the **Rabbit in the Moon** in the East will manifest this kind of luck for you.

MARRIED COUPLES BEWARE!!!

While there will be plenty of love and romance in 2021, it will not always be the kind that brings happiness. The year's chart also features the *Flower of Romance Star*. Unfortunately, it is the "external" version of this star – making all marriages vulnerable as there will be too much temptation from outside. Innocent flirtations can get out of hand, after-work drinks with colleagues or out-of-town business conferences can lead to inappropriate entanglements, spouses with the seven-year itch could be tempted to act on it. This is a year when those who are married should pay more attention to their other halves.

The *External Star of Romance* often affect those who have grown to take their marriage for granted. As long as you realise it, you can start taking measures to make things right. But what if an affair has already started?

CURE: We advise that when this troublesome star is present, married couples should make an effort to display symbols of marital stability and happiness in the home. All married couples should have the **Marriage Happiness Ducks** in the home, in the SW, East or center. Each can also carry the **Enhancing Relationships Amulet** to protect against third parties elbowing their way in and "crowding" the marriage.

Displaying the **"Rabbit in the Moon" Love Enhancer** in the home is also an excellent protective measure against stars that affect marital peace and happiness. In 2021, all couples can safeguard their marriage by displaying the Moon Rabbit with the full moon in the East part of their home. For those who suspect their spouse is already cheating, you can call on the help of **Kurukulle**, the powerful Goddess of Love. Invoking her presence in your life imbues you with her talent for enchantment, giving you your power back when it comes to your spouse and your marriage. You can display her **Banner of Love** or carry the **Red Tara Home Protection Amulet** – this powerful talisman designed with her image and all her implements of love will repair damage already done to your marriage, while strengthening the bond between you and your spouse. Kurukulle's powers of magnetism will also make it difficult for others to adversely affect your marriage.

We also advise chanting her mantra daily:
OM KURUKULLE HRIH SOHA (21 times or 108 times)

STUDY LUCK IN 2021

To enhance study luck in 2021, students should call on the help of **Manjushri**, the Buddha of Wisdom. Manjushri with his wisdom sword slices through all ignorance in the mind, enhancing one's wisdom and knowledge. Invoking his help benefits not just students and those studying for exams, but also anyone needing to make important decisions and life choices. He clears the mind to make way for effective and efficient accumulation of knowledge – so that "your knowledge is vast, and your understanding complete". This year we have designed a **Manjushri Home Amulet** for scholars and students to place on their study desk. Manjushri's seed syllable is "DHIH" and chanting this repeatedly in one breath until you run out of breath is the best way to invoke his presence.

You can also chant Manjushri's wisdom mantra:
OM AH RAPA CHA NA DHIH

Make it a habit to chant his mantra either 21 times or 108 times (1 mala) before you sleep each night, or when you can find some quiet time during the day. We suggest you get yourself a **Manjushri Wisdom Mala** which you reserve specially for this purpose – chanting only Manjushri's Wisdom Mantra. This sharpens the mala's power and effectiveness when it comes to study luck, as the energies you direct into the mala as you chant becomes concentrated, making it more and more potent the more you use it.

HEALTH LUCK IN 2021

The Illness Star has flown into the North, the sector of the Rat. This affects all those born in Rat years, but also those whose main doors or bedrooms are located in the North of the home, or those who spend a lot of time in the North sector. Those afflicted with sickness or health problems should have the **Healing Deer** in the North.

Health risks continue to look like a threat going into 2021 so we have designed several potent health and protective talismans to keep everyone safe.

Our **mantra ring** this year features Medicine Buddha's mantra on the outside and Vairocana's mantra on the inside. Medicine Buddha comes to the aid of anyone who is sick and who calls to him for help. Vairocana is the Buddha that protects against contagious diseases. COVID-19 has been a life-altering phenomenon for the whole world throughout the last year, and as we move into 2021, it does not look like things will revert quite back to normal. We need to continue to practise vigilance following new guidelines as they get discovered to keep safe. Mask up, keep your social distance and get used to a new way of living.

The science of feng shui meanwhile always advocates protection before enhancement, so we strongly advise everyone irrespective of their animal signs to always wear or carry health and protective amulets. It can literally save your life!

The **Medicine Buddha-Vairocana Mantra Ring** is excellent to help keep you safe during these strange times and troubled times.

This year we also strongly recommend the **Health Talisman with Tortoise and Snake**. The Tortoise and Snake are two spiritual creatures associated with longevity, known for their potent powers to heal. The tortoise provides stability both in physical and mental health, while the Snake represents control over the nagas, spirits that can cause ill health and sickness when they are left to their own mischievous devices.

All signs whose element luck tables indicate a poor health category should also place these health cures near to them or carry as portable amulets.

Luck of the Dog in 2021

Chapter 2

- Fire Dog – 15 & 75 years
- Wood Dog – 27 & 87 years
- Water Dog – 39 years
- Metal Dog – 51 years
- Earth Dog – 63 years

ELEMENT LUCK OF THE DOG IN 2021

The element luck chart of the Dog is lukewarm in 2021. While there is little to get excited about when it comes to your element luck this year, you do however have good life force, and often this is the category of luck that matters the most. When you have a good level of life force, it gives you the strength and impetus to keep striving for success. Even if other categories may not look promising, when your life force is strong, it suggests you can overcome whatever obstacles come your way. 2021 may not produce neccesarily levels of success you usually aim for, but it can certainly be a year for building a strong foundation.

An important thing for the Dog is to lift the levels of your spirit essence in 2021, which is weak. A weak spirit essence makes you more light-eared, more sensitive and more easily influenced by others. It lowers your defences against spirit harm and makes you more susceptible to being manipulated by others. It is vitally important then for the Dog sign this year to strengthen this category of your luck by carrying **protective talismans** as well as the **"Om" Dakini Spirit Enhancing Amulet**.

You can also use element therapy by having strategically placed feng shui remedies that activate the necessary elements. When you do this, you will

ELEMENT LUCK OF

	WOOD DOG 87/27 years	FIRE DOG 75/15 years	EARTH DOG 63 years
Life Force	good G	good G	good G
Health	neutral Gx	good G	very good GG
Wealth	very bad xx	very good GG	neutral Gx
Success	neutral Gx	neutral Gx	neutral Gx
Spirit Essence	bad x	bad x	bad x

THE DOG IN 2021

METAL DOG 51 years	WATER DOG 39 years	2021 Element
good O	good O	Earth
excellent OOO	very bad XX	Earth
bad X	excellent OOO	Metal
neutral OX	neutral OX	Water
bad X	bad X	Fire

be strengthening the elements themselves, hence bringing vital vigorous energy to your living space. By familiarizing yourself with the different elements needed for each of the luck categories, you do a better job of activating the different categories of luck near you.

To boost your spirit essence, you need Earth element enhancers, so for the Dog in 2021, surrounding yourself with Earth energy in the form of natural crystals and crystal balls, as well as wearing natural precious or semi-precious gemstones, will help raise your levels of spirit essence.

You should also make more of an effort to be happy. Surround yourself with positive people. These are the emotional ingredients of powerful spiritual energy. Engage in activities that bring a smile to your face. All this will draw out your inner vitality and help you rise to the top of your game. Spend time with friends who build you up. Avoid pessimists who undermine your confidence.

When your spirit essence is strong, it makes you feel motivated and invigorated. This reawakens interest in the work you do and adds sparkle to your social life. A good level of spirit essence always brings greater enjoyment to all your relationships.

When you get hit by the blues, do not to succumb to energies that make you feel down. Remember that we create the energies that surround us; we create our own reality. When you feel boredom manifesting in your life, know that this is simply mirroring the element combinations in your chart. You can change how you feel simply by maneuvering the combinations of elements around you.

The Dog in 2021 needs to apply element therapy to its living space to improve its element luck. The main problem area is your spirit essence, which affects your mood and disposition. To fix this, engage in things that make you happy. Surround yourself with people who make you feel good. Avoid pessimists. Thicken your skin.

Your success category meanwhile has a neutral showing. What this means is that your success in 2021 will be entirely up to you. How much you attain will not depend on outside factors, so you must not expect opportunities to fall into your lap. You have to go out looking for them. Self-starter Dogs can do very well this year, but the lapdog variety who expect things handed to them could end up feeling very sorry for themselves.

All Dogs need the **Windhorse** this year – this is the symbol that will do the most to boost your personal *lung ta,* which controls your success luck. You make success this year, so strive to be your own ...or and to keep the company of those who ...vate you and make you feel worthy and good ...out yourself. The more self-confidence you can garner, the better will be your success luck.

The Dog is the most loyal of the Chinese Zodiac. You are happiest when helping others and when you have a noble cause to sink your teeth into. Find something to motivate you this year. For the Dog, when someone else's well-being is at stake is when you will fight the hardest. So if you need someone to fight for, go adopt a cause.

WEALTH LUCK FOR THE DIFFERENT DOGS

Wealth luck differs for the different element Dogs, but especially benefits the **39-year-old Water Dog** in 2021. This Dog enjoys excellent element wealth luck, which suggests that financially, this Dog will be secure, and its wealth can grow. The **75-year-old Fire Dog** also has very good element wealth luck. To take full advantage, this Dog should display the **Tree Bringing 3 Kinds of Wealth** in its living space; this will add growth energy to its wealth potential, boosting career and investment luck, and for some, even attract a windfall.

The **63-year-old Earth Dog** has neutral element wealth luck, suggesting that while you could be doing better financially, you are not in trouble. Even if cash flow becomes tight, you find a way to cope.

The **51-year-old Metal Dog** has a less robust indication in your wealth luck category. The advice for this Dog is to steer clear of risky investments. For you, the best strategy is to maintain a sufficiently diversified portfolio. Do not succumb to taking financial risks, no matter how irresistible, as luck is not with you when it comes to money matters in 2021.

The **27-year-old and 87-year-old Wood Dogs** have their wealth category at a VERY BAD level, so this is a warning to take serious steps to preserve wealth this year. Avoid taking risks when it comes to money. This is not a year for frivolous expenditures. Unexpected expenses could crop up, disrupting your personal financial plan for the year. Be conservative, do not spend in excess, and limit your exuberance when it comes to spending money. These Dogs need the **"Hum" Dakini Wealth Protection Amulet** to safeguard their wealth.

HEALTH OF THE DOG

The only Dog with anything serious to worry about when it comes to health is the **39-year-old Water Dog**. For this Dog, you should pay more attention to your physical wellbeing. Go for regular check-ups. If you vell for any reason, get it looked at. Do not alth concerns to a point when it is too late to do ng about it. While you may be active and feeling s a fiddle, never take your health for granted, especially this year.

This Dog should carry the **Health Talisman with Health Mantras** and have the **Medicine Buddha & 7 Sugatas Gau** near you. Be mindful not to expose yourself to infectious viruses; post COVID19, you must absolutely not take any risks when it comes to contagious diseases. If there are quarantine recommendations in place, follow them! Don't be foolhardy and think you are invincible, because this year, health-wise, you are not.

FIRE DOG 15 year old	
life force	good G
health	good G
wealth	very good GG
success	neutral Gx
spirit essence	bad x

THE 15-YEAR-OLD FIRE DOG

The teenaged Fire Dog is happy and well-balanced and less prone to teenager angst sometimes prevalent in children of this age. Often jovial and even-tempered, this Dog gets along well with both peers and parents. This Dog has great empathy with others, and are exceedingly loyal, sometimes naively so. But its good nature attracts equally dependable friends, so this Dog will often have a solid support system for whenever the going gets tough.

At 15, this Dog is likely in the midst of its school career, and possibly taking important exams for the first time. But because they are so well put together, there is little worry that things will not go smoothly. In fact, the Dog is likely to sail through its adolescence with joy and ease. While academia may not be the only important goal for the Dog, this young Dog takes its schoolwork and school career seriously, so as a parent to this teenager, you are unlikely to have problems here.

The Dog is a spirited and outgoing sign, and highly protective of those it considers its "clan". If this Dog is an older sibling in the family, he or she will relish being big brother or sister, sometimes even stepping in as an alternate parent or carer. This teenaged Dog will be independent but thrives on praise. Unlike other teenagers, this one will not be so embarrassed when given parent-cuddles in public.

2021 is a highly promising year for this young Dog. Health luck is good, suggesting a strong disposition and an unwavering spirit. Life force is also good, which provides a strong inner drive to work towards meaningful goals and aspirations. Of all the Dogs, this young Dog has one of the most promising luck profiles this year, and those taking important exams can do very well indeed.

For this Dog, the key is to continue working hard. You are at an exciting stage in life, when anything is possible. Keep your options open. Keep up your various and possibly many different co-curricular activities. You don't have to make up your mind yet which direction you want to take. The future is bright but there is no need to clarify a path just yet. For now, focus on doing well in your exams and continuing to learn new things and to hone new skills.

The 15-year-old Dog benefits from the **Manjushri "Dhih" Scholastic Amulet** and **Manjushri's Gau**. Buddha Manjushri will imbue you with his wisdom and aid you greatly in your scholastic career. You should also carry the **"Om" Dakini Spirit Enhancing Amulet** to lift this category of your luck.

WOOD DOG 27 year old	
life force	good o
health	neutral ox
wealth	very bad xx
success	neutral ox
spirit essence	bad x

THE 27-YEAR-OLD WOOD DOG

The **27-year-old Wood Dog** has an average element luck forecast. You have good life force, but all other categories are neutral or negative. This suggests that this is a year to be careful, to play it safe, and to maintain the status quo instead of striving for changes that are too sudden or too big. Stay on your current path and leave the really big decisions for another time. Don't tempted to jump from the frying pan into the fire. This is a year when the devil you know is better than the one you don't.

In terms of creating new wealth, this is not a good time to be thinking in this direction, as this is not where your current destiny lies. You are at the planning stage of your life, and this is a time to gain experience and store up observations for the future. Clarify what you want to do with your life. It is not yet time to be thinking of making big money or exploiting big opportunities.

Focus on learning about yourself and about what you really want and are good at. Work at accumulating experience that can benefit you in the future. But do not allow yourself to stagnate; instead be watchful and attentive and keep striving to improve your skills.

This Dog benefits from **Vajrasattva's Mantra Wand**. Filled with Vajrasattva's mantra, this wand will remove obstacles to good fortune and aid you in making the most of the coming year. Keep as a wand talisman on your work desk or carry in your bag.

For those of you pursuing success in your career, we suggest that you carry the **Income Generating Amulet**. This will help balance out

Income Generating Amulet

the poor wealth reading in your chart and put you on firm footing to get ahead in your work and career.

WATER DOG 39 year old	
life force	good G
health	very bad XX
wealth	excellent GGG
success	neutral GX
spirit essence	bad X

THE 39-YEAR-OLD WATER DOG

The **39-year-old Water Dog** enjoys excellent wealth luck but very poor health luck. This is a year when health issues can cause serious problems that make you and your loved ones worry, so do watch your health more carefully than usual. Don't put off a trip to the doctor's or seeking professional medical advice if you think you need it. When it comes to your health this year, better safe than sorry. If it turns out to be nothing, be thankful. But it is always better to check than leave something to develop to a point when it becomes rather too late.

In terms of lifestyle, make time for regular exercise. Eat sensibly and get enough rest. Those working in stressful jobs should find a way to periodically switch off to take your mind off things. It is important to de-stress, especially if you start to find that a lot of your waking moments are stressful ones. If you don't have a hobby, maybe think of having one, something to take your mind somewhere else and to engage you in different ways. It may also enlarge your social circle and bring you into contact with fresh new ideas. This year it benefits to expand the horizons in your life a little more.

Financially, the Water Dog is in a very comfortable place as your Wealth luck is at an excellent level! You need not worry about this category of luck as the element combinations are firmly in your favour here. Some of you may even benefit from gaining a sudden windfall this year, so do not forget to buy the odd lottery. Or you can come into some unexpected inheritance. No matter how the extra money comes, you can be sure that financially, you are comfortable this year.

This Dog benefits from health enhancers. Carry the **Medicine Buddha Amulet** or **Medicine Buddha's Mantra Wand**. These will help you guard against illness; or if you are already suffering from ill health of any kind, it will help you recover. For money luck, this Dog should have the **Winning Chip Talisman** – this will activate the exciting wealth possibilities in your chart!

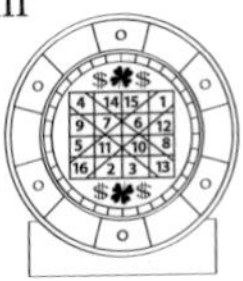

Winning Chip Talisman

To improve career success and luck in business, carry the **"White Tiger" Constellation Lucky Charms**. This will shield you from the pitfalls of working life while ensuring you keep moving forward and upward both in rank and financially.

METAL DOG 51 year old	
life force	good o
health	excellent ooo
wealth	bad x
success	neutral ox
spirit essence	bad x

THE 51-YEAR-OLD METAL DOG

The 51-year-old Metal Dog enjoys excellent health this year. This is a great indication as it suggests you have the energy to take on anything you wish to. Whether your goals are physical, intellectual or monetary in nature, you have the energy to go after them. You are operating at an impressive level of productivity, and you are as robust physically as you are mentally.

But wealth luck is not at quite the same level; in fact, wealth has a negative showing, so while you can accomplish much this year, your wealth goals may fall short. This is not a year to take financial risks. When it comes to money, this Dog should stay conservative. Have enough in the bank for a rainy day. Be wary of investments or opportunities that seem too good to be true, as they probably are.

This year, turn your focus towards non-monetary goals. Big financial success is likely to elude you, stressing out those of you who have your own money at stake. Do not gamble, avoid speculation, and do not risk your own money. The only way to make money for this Dog this year is through old-fashioned hard work. Don't be too hard on yourself if you don't achieve the results you are looking for. 2021 is not a prolific year when it comes to wealth, so draw satisfaction from other aspects of your life.

This Dog benefits from displaying **Wealth Cabinets**. These wealth enhancer symbolize your prosperity accumulating and activates an aspect of your element luck that needs help in 2021. Fill your wealth cabinets with Iching coins and miniature ingots, or even real coins and real money! Place in the NW or West. You also benefit from carrying the **Asset Wealth Bull Talisman** to activate for long term prosperity luck and to protect against your investments losing value.

EARTH DOG 63 year old	
life force	good G
health	very good GG
wealth	neutral Gx
success	neutral Gx
spirit essence	bad x

THE 63-YEAR-OLD EARTH DOG

This Dog can look forward to a moderate year. Health luck is very good, which gives you the energy you need to pursue what you want, but your wealth luck is merely neutral, which means while there may be money to be made, it will not be big money. You will be financially secure so your mind can rest easy here, but you should work at not deriving your happiness not from how well you are doing financially, but from other things, as money will not be your strong suit in 2021.

The Earth Dog has always been a champion of rights for every cause from the poor to the sick or underprivileged, and this year, nothing brings you more satisfaction than being able to do your part, no matter how small.

All Dogs are natural social workers who enjoy nothing better than to do good in this world; but this is particularly so with the Earth Dog. You are Mother Earth personified, the most likely to champion noble causes, to turn vegetarian or vegan, to condemn others for their cavalier attitudes to the environment...
So turn your sights to making a difference this year.

This Dog in 2021 needs something to galvanize it into action. When you have something you believe in to work towards, you become productive, efficient and more importantly, happy. When you are happy, you lift your inner spirits, which in turn boosts your spirit essence. Your low spirit essence is your biggest worry this year, so anything that can successfully lift this will help clear away many obstacles to success this year.

This Dog should carry the **"Om" Dakini Spirit Enhancing Amulet** to lift your spirit essence. For better wealth prospects, this Dog should display the **Ox Finding Hidden Wealth** to unlock the hidden wealth luck of the year.

FIRE DOG 75 year old	
life force	good G
health	good G
wealth	very good GG
success	neutral Gx
spirit essence	bad x

THE 75-YEAR-OLD FIRE DOG

The 75-year-old Fire Dog enjoys good health and very good wealth luck. This Dog has very good wealth luck and good health luck in 2021, so there is little standing in your way to making this a very pleasant year. The Fire Dog is the more dramatic of your Dog siblings, and you do exceptionally well in the limelight. Those born under this sign make good orators and public personalities. 2021 bodes well for you as you are helped by your element luck, but you need to ensure you do not allow yourself to be overly influenced by too many different quarters with different agendas.

This fiery Dog has the kind of destiny which gains you many followers but also many detractors, and in 2021, you need to play your cards carefully to retain the favor of your supporters. It can be a slippery slope, as your spirit essence is weak. You need to work at improving this aspect of your luck. Don't be overly impulsive in your decisions, and plan before making brash moves. Your Fire element gives you the inner passion you need to do your work, but it can also be your undoing, if you allow it to rage out of control. Plan your moves, back up decisions with solid reasoning and avoid acting on pure impulse.

This Dog benefits from invoking the Buddha Manjushri. Keep **Manjushri's Gau** near you. He is the Buddha of Wisdom and with his blessings, he will help ensure all decisions made are sage ones that lead to positive and beneficial outcomes. You should also carry the **"Om" Dakini Spirit Enhancing Amulet.**

Four Pillars Chart 2021

Chapter 3

FOUR PILLARS CHART 2021

An important indicator of the potential of any year is the Four Pillars chart of the year. This reveals the impact of the five elements of the year. When all five elements are present, it indicates a balance, a preferred situation. In feng shui, we are always striving for balance, and when something is out of balance, we always endeavor to bring things back into balance by introducing the missing element. This year, the chart

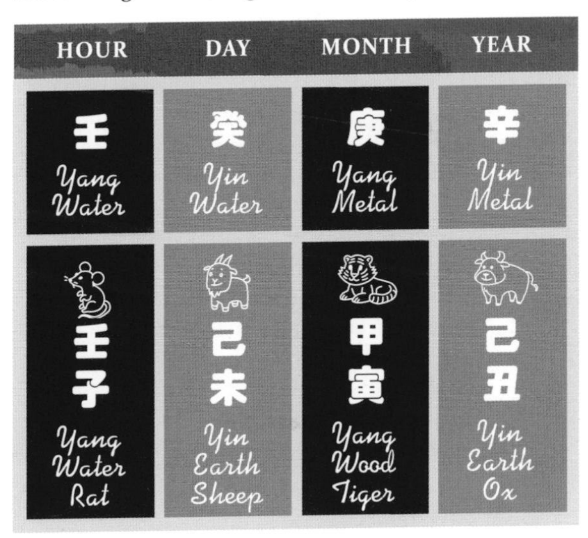

This year's Four Pillars chart lacks Fire, the element that signifies wealth luck.

is obviously missing Fire, the element that indicates WEALTH LUCK, so the year lacks opportunities to make money.

However, the eight characters in the Four Pillars – made up of 4 heavenly stems and 4 earthly branches – are not the only elements present. The interaction of these elements, depending on where and how they are positioned within the chart, generates a set of hidden elements as well as special stars. We use this chapter to analyse each part of this year's Four Pillars chart, and mention the most significant findings.

2021's Paht Chee chart indicates a strong self-element of Water, which boosts competitive energies and puts everyone on edge. Friends become foes when the stakes are raised, so this is a year to constantly watch one's back. The year's chart is unbalanced; it is missing the vital element of FIRE, which represents wealth and financial success. It is thus a year when it will be difficult to make much headway in the creation of new wealth. Profits may take a long time to get realized and there are few speculative gains to be made.

Prosperity comes with hard work rather than with a stroke of luck. This is definitely not a year to strike it rich via the lottery.

Here is a closer look at the most important indications this year:

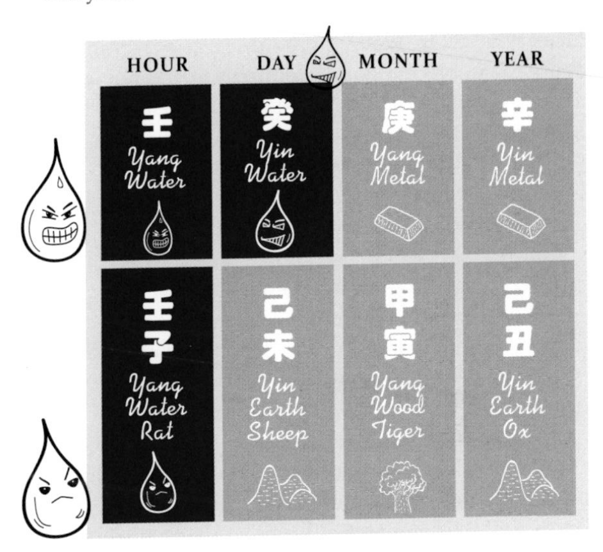

There appears to be way too much Water in this year's chart.

A YEAR OF STRONG WATER indicating a competitive year

First, the self-element of the year is Strong Water. It is a year when rivalry becomes enhanced and when politics can get unscrupulous. Watch your back and reserve your trust for your very innermost circle. Indeed, even your inner circle could let you down if the circumstances dictate. Betrayals happen of their own accord, sometimes without the guilty party's conscious intention. Learn to forgive and move on but protect yourself by being more careful and by putting safeguards in place. Remove temptation where you can and stay close to all you are working with.

PROTECTION: Those in business are advised to carry the **Kuan Kung on Horseback Anti-Betrayal Amulet**. This will protect you against the betrayal of others and being let down by people whom you trust. It keeps you prepared for whatever the winds and waters bring your way.

In any competitive endeavour, it could well feel like a fight to the death. Diplomatic compromises will be difficult to achieve, and different factions and interest groups find it harder to reach win-win scenarios. But it is nevertheless important to try. Sometimes being the bigger person will help; but recognize when you have to fight and when you don't. Indeed, do not mistakenly think you are in fact being the magnanimous one when you are being taken for a fool. It is a year when it is prudent to carry protection always. The **28 Hums Protection Amulet** is an excellent all-round amulet that will safeguard you from all kinds of harm.

SOLUTION: The excess of Water energy in the chart needs to be resolved. Use **WOOD energy** to weaken the excess Water. Having plenty of greenery and live plants in your living space will help re-balance the energies and will also bring vital growth energy to a year which lacks the presence of the *Lap Chun*, or "Spring".

This year, having plenty of plants and Wood energy around you will help soak up the excess Water in the year's chart.

BALANCE OF YIN & YANG

Second, there are two Yang pillars and two Yin Pillars. There is thus a good mix between energetic periods and restive ones, with no dominance of work over play, or vice versa. The Yang Month and Hour Pillars bring great vitality, while the Yin Year and Day Pillars bring balance. There should be more than enough strength to propel positive chi forward and upward. People in general are open to different viewpoints. If negative energies can be kept under control and sufficiently subdued, the year is then able to propel forward, benefitting many.

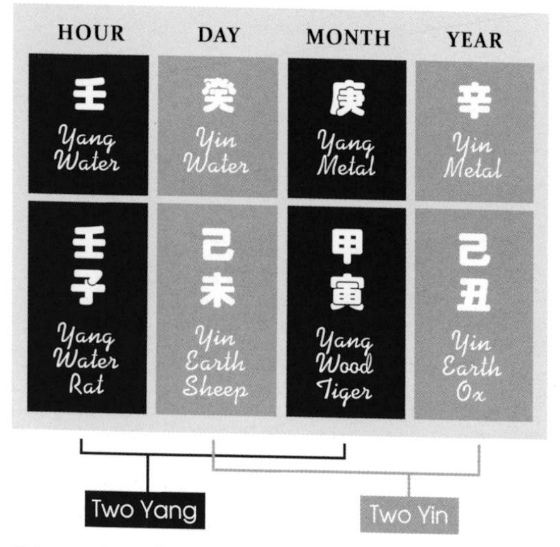

This year there is good balance between Yang and Yin in the year's Four Pillars chart.

CLASH OF SHEEP WITH OX

indicating strong conflict energy

Third, there is a clash of SHEEP with OX in the Earth Branches. This clash between two Earth animals suggests that the clash will be between leaders. Earth is the element that represents leadership and rank, thus animosity will likely be between those who are in charge. But because those in power are especially strong this year, fighting can become ferocious, with the damage dealt far-reaching. There will be strong clashes between the leaders of nations.

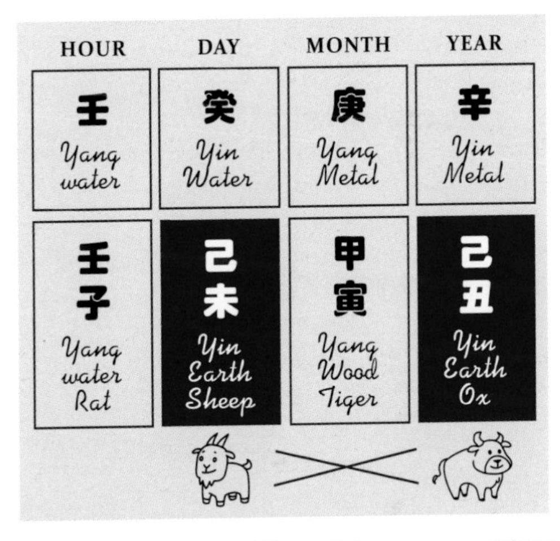

The clash between Ox and Sheep brings many problems to the year, especially between those who are in charge and everyone else, who could end up as collateral damage.

Within family units, because the clash Occurs in the Day Pillar, there is likely to be strong conflict between spouses.

SOLUTION: There may be more marital problems in 2021 with the Sheep in the Self-Spouse pillar clashing with the Year pillar. In the family unit, this coupled with the presence of the *External Flower of Romance* star brings all kinds of problems to husband and wife. Every home this year should have the **"Rabbit in the Moon" Love Enhancer** and better still if both husband and wife carry the **Enhancing Relationships Amulet**. Recognize when an outsider is trying to make trouble in your marriage, and refrain from siding with a third party over your spouse, no matter how much your husband or wife may be annoying you. When you allow an outsider into the mix, this year, such troubles can escalate very quickly.

Enhancing Relationships Amulet

SPECIAL LINK BETWEEN RAT & OX

bringing creativity and inventiveness

Fourth, there is however a very strong affinity between RAT and OX in the Earthly Branches of the Year and Hour Pillar. This is a heaven sent because it serves to repair some of the damage resulting from the Ox-Sheep clash. The Year Pillar of the Ox forms a soulmate pairing with the Hour Pillar of the Rat, which means there is a good beginning and a good ending to the year, what the Chinese refer to as having a head and tail, a suggestion that things that

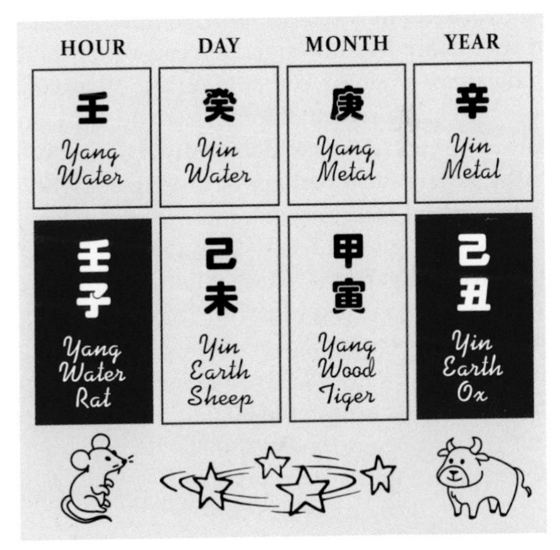

The Rat and Ox in this year's chart form a very special affinity, bringing relationship and completion luck.

get started have a good chance to reach satisfactory completion. The two signs of Rat and Ox are extremely harmonious together, generating the *House of Cleverness and Creativity,* with the Rat starting and the Ox completing. This endows the year with wonderful ingenuity and inventiveness.

The presence of the Rat & Ox in the year's Four Pillars suggests a year when true friendship means something.

These two signs are also a secret-friend pair, indicating **good friendship luck** through the year. While there are indications of strong competition and rivalry, there is also much potential for firm friendships, and opportunities for friends to demonstrate their loyalties and allegiance. A year perhaps of finding out who one's true friends are.

ENHANCER: Get the **"Perfect Partnerships to Attract Big Wealth" Enhancer**. This enhancer featuring the Ox and Rat will boost all the positive indications of this combination. Display in a prominent area in the home; in the living room, or near the dining room where you spend a lot of time. The number "8" on the Ox activates for the missing wealth luck of the year.

NO PROSPERITY LUCK INDICATED
... but there is hidden wealth

Fifth, there is MISSING WEALTH. Fire which represents wealth is completely missing from the main chart. What this indicates is that it will be difficult to make money. New businesses will take time getting off the ground, sales will be slow, industries that are shrinking will continue to do so, while their replacements will take time to take flight. Profit margins get squeezed as information becomes more and more freely available, and technology continues to disrupt at breakneck pace. This year, if one wants to stay afloat, it is vitally important to keep up with the world that is so rapidly changing around us.

While there will be results and completions, it will nevertheless feel like an interim year, because we are at the beginning end of a new cycle, and not quite at the close of the current period. 2021 represents the second animal sign of the cycle after the new decade last year opened with the Rat, and we are heading towards the end of Period 8, and the beginning of Period 9, but we are not quite there yet.

There is a lack of obvious wealth in 2021, but those who look harder can find gold. This year, there is HIDDEN WEALTH brought by the sign of the TIGER.

While WEALTH luck may be lacking, there is however HIDDEN WEALTH brought by the TIGER. This will bring some respite, and keep us tided over, but it is wealth that comes in its own time rather than overnight. What this means is that 2021 is a year when we can lay the foundations for future wealth, but we must not get our hopes up for immediate results.

That the hidden wealth star is brought by the Tiger bodes well for friends of the Tiger – the Dog and especially the Horse.

The Dog enjoys one *Small Auspicious Star* from the 24 mountains chart, while the Horse enjoys not one but *TWO Big Auspicious Stars*, together with a *Golden Deity Star*. These two astrological allies of the big cat are lucky in this respect in terms of money-making prospects, although all signs can boost wealth luck with suitable activators and enhancers.

THE COLOUR FOR WEALTH: The wearing of the most auspicious colour of the spectrum RED will bring significant added benefits in 2021. Red is the colour which represents ultimate YANG, which serves to boost the year's vitality, but will do double duty in enhancing the missing Wealth element of the year. Red in 2021 stands for WEALTH, so wearing this colour as part of your wardrobe or accessories will give you a boost of good fortune. You should also carry the **"Increase Your Wealth Luck" Gold Talisman Card** featuring the God of Wealth Tsai Shen Yeh seated on a Tiger. This will attract wealth of the kind that keeps increasing and will help you tap the hidden wealth luck of the year.

You can also display the **Bejewelled God of Wealth sitting on a Tiger** in figurine form in the home.

Bejewelled God of Wealth sitting on a Tiger

Before the New Year arrives, make sure you get our specially created **Red Wealth Wallet** featuring the Wealth Ox. It is auspicious each year to change to a new wallet and especially lucky to take some money from your old wallet and transfer it over to your new wallet. Doing so for this year will ensure you take some of the energy of last year, and carry it over into the following year. In 2021 you definitely want to do this, as the previous Year of the Rat carried two *Lap Chuns*, or two "Springs" while this year has none.

Keep the lights in your home brightly turned on throughout the year, especially in the WEST sector, which plays host to the Prosperity Star #8.

POWERFUL SPIRITUAL ENHANCER: For Wealth Luck that is potent and long-lasting, an excellent ritual to incorporate into your life is the **White Dzambala Ritual**. Invite in **White Dzambala and the Four Dakinis** who pull in

wealth from the four directions. Display in a respectful place in the home and recite White Dzambala's mantra as regularly as you can.

***White Dzambala's Mantra*:**
Om Padma Krodha Arya Dzambala
Hridaya Hum Phat

When you gaze upon him and chant his mantra regularly, he manifests great riches in your life and attracts incredible opportunities that can bring wealth of a big meaningful and lasting kind.

INVITE IN THE ROOSTER: The Rooster brings the #8 Wealth Star in 2021, so it is extremely auspicious to have many images of Roosters in the home this year. The Rooster is also the symbol that ensures politicking is kept to a minimum, protecting against harmful gossip and slander. The Rooster is also wonderful for protecting the marriage, preventing any troublesome third party from trying to come between husband and wife.

Rooster with Crown

There are many benefits to displaying the Rooster this year; indeed, it may be a good time to start collecting Roosters, made of different colours and in different materials if you wish. You can also display Rooster Art in the home, which is most auspicious. Display in the West part of the home.

Our new **Rooster with Crown** this year has been embellished with powerful symbols of protection and good fortune, to ensure the negative energies of the year cannot harm you. It features the "Anti Evil-Eye" to protect against jealousy, the Double Dorje for wisdom in decision making and the powerful "Hum" seed syllable for strong protection. Its powerful feathers sweep away all harmful energies and its crown symbolizes holding dominion over the year.

LUCKY SPECIAL STARS OF 2021

Sixth, there are two potentially VERY AUSPICIOUS stars in the year's Four Pillars chart. These are seriously good stars noted for being strong and very explicit in their beneficial influence. These stars have the capability of bringing incredible good fortune to those who know how to activate them correctly, while making sure the positive aspects of their influences materialize.

These stars impact different animal signs differently and in varying degrees, but are nevertheless very beneficial for all signs. Note that you will need to wear or carry the relevant activators to ensure that you make the most of the positive influence of these stars.

THE STAR OF PROSPECTS

brings many new opportunities

This star brought by the Earthly Branch of Rat in the Hour Pillar with the self-element of Water indicates many new opportunities in the coming year. This favourable star conjures up a very special energy that rewards determination and staying power, resonating

HOUR	DAY	MONTH	YEAR
壬 Yang Water	癸 Yin Water	庚 Yang Metal	辛 Yin Metal
壬 子 Yang Water Rat	己 未 Yin Earth Sheep	甲 寅 Yang Wood Tiger	己 丑 Yin Earth Ox

The Star of Prospects brings many new opportunities in the coming year.

with the Ox sign of the year, a reminder that those who retain their passion for success will benefit from its presence. This star suggests there is nothing that cannot be achieved for those prepared to work hard. The more ambitious one is, the further one can go this year.

STAR OF PROSPECTS: To activate this star in your favour, keep an **image of an Ox** near you. We suggest the **Bejewelled Asset Bull** to magnify wealth luck and to ensure the hard work you put in meets with proportionate success. This bull has been designed with an auspicious saddle in red, the colour that signifies wealth in 2021, wearing a harness of coins and stepping on a pile of wealth and ingots, symbolizing the accumulation of assets.

This beautiful enhancer will allow you to accumulate everything you work for and ensure you do not spend everything you earn. It will also increase the opportunities that come your way.

THE STAR OF POWERFUL MENTORS
brings Benefactor Luck

The Star of Powerful Mentors which was also in last year's chart makes another appearance in 2021. This star is brought by the OX in the Year Pillar and the Heavenly Stem of YANG METAL in the Month Pillar. This star is especially beneficial for the younger generation, who have the auspicious luck of influential people turning up in their lives to help them, giving them meaningful advice and powerful support.

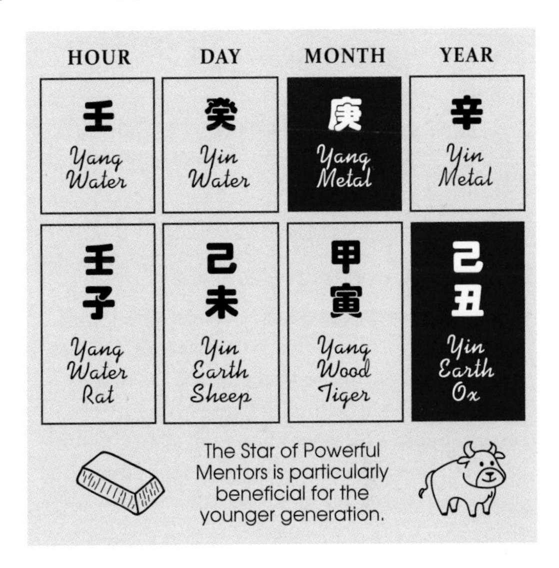

For students hungry for success, mentors will open doors to scholarship, and teachers will provide fabulous inspiration and motivation. Opportunities abound and there will be unseen hands supporting you. Those just starting out in your careers can find a mentor figure to guide you and to show you the ropes. An influential boss could fast-track your promotion up the ranks.

ACTIVATE THE STAR OF POWERFUL MENTORS: Bring this star to life by displaying **Kuan Kung** in the home. You can also display near to you work or study desk. Another powerful activator for this star is the **Nobleman with Qui Ren Talisman**. The benefits of this special star are immense, so it is worth activating. It brings help from the heavens, manifesting someone in your life with the wish and means to help you, and ensures those with this kind of power stay firmly on your side.

AFFLICTIVE STARS OF 2021

There are two unlucky stars brought by the Four Pillars chart of the year. These, when not attended to with relevant cures, can wreak a lot of havoc and create a lot of misfortune, but their ill influence can be avoided if you take special note and address them.

THE AGGRESSIVE SWORD STAR
is a Double-Edged Sword

The Aggressive Sword Star formed by the Yin Water in the Heavenly Stem of the Day Pillar and the Earthly Branch of Ox in the Year Pillar suggests a year of

The Aggressive Sword Star can be both good and bad.

intense aggression. It indicates the strengthening of the underdog's chi, so it points to a rise of revolutionary fervour, people revolting against authority. Strikes continue, spawning groups around the globe to walk similar paths. Protests advocating for greater equality, non-discrimination, fighting against police brutality and other social injustices continue to pick up steam. There will be anger, passion, rioting and violence.

At its pinnacle, the presence of this star suggests the emergence of powerful leaders on opposing sides, or of highly influential opposition to established leaders. It suggests the rise of a people who seize power by fair means or foul. The name of this star is ***Yang Ren***, which describes "***yang essence sharp blade that inflicts damage***". This is a star with great potential for either very good or very bad influences to materialize during the year, although generally, the influence tends to be more negative than positive. There is risk of revolution and of the toppling of unpopular leaders in power.

The Aggressive Sword Star brings potential for violence & bloodshed. This star must be strongly subdued.

In this year's chart, the *Star of Aggressive Sword* is created by the strong YIN WATER of the DAY pillar, with the presence of the OX in the YEAR pillar. Here, note that the WATER element is strong in the chart, making the presence of the Aggressive Sword much more negative. It indicates that those emerging as leaders for the underdog in 2021 will end up being heavy-handed and quick-tempered. They may be charismatic but they will also be strong-willed, conceited, arrogant, overbearing and self-centered - all nasty traits that spell the potential for bloodshed and violence wherever they emerge. There is real danger of this this year!

CURE: To shield against the harmful effects of the Aggressive Sword Star, the best remedy is a powerful spiritual Stupa. The **Kumbum Stupa** is especially beneficial as it contains one hundred holy images, invoking the protection of all the world's Wisdom Protectors. This Stupa will ensure that all family members living within the home stay protected against aggression or violence of any kind. It is also a good idea to wear or carry the **28 Hums Protection Wheel Amulet** at all times.

Kumbum Stupa

THE FLOWER OF ROMANCE STAR (EXTERNAL) *makes marriages vulnerable*

This star is sometimes confused with the *Peach Blossom Star* because it addresses the destiny of love; but while both influence love and romance, they are very different in their effects. When the Flower of Romance is present, it suggests love blossoms easily, but it is not the kind of love that leads to marriage and family. It indicates instead the possibility of extramarital affairs, bringing stress and unhappiness to married couples. There is also a difference between ***internal*** and ***external romance***, and in this year of the Ox, it is unfortunately the latter that prevails. So the year

HOUR	DAY	MONTH	YEAR
壬 Yang Water	癸 Yin Water	庚 Yang Metal	辛 Yin Metal
壬 子 Yang Water Rat	己 未 Yin Earth Sheep	甲 寅 Yang Wood Tiger	己 丑 Yin Earth Ox

The External Flower of Romance Star brings stress and risk of infidelity to marriages.

is likely to see increased occurrences of infidelity and break-ups of marriages.

Marriages are vulnerable to the External Flower of Romance this year.

The SHEEP in the Day Pillar and RAT of the Hour Pillar indicate the presence of the *External Romance Star,* making all marriages vulnerable to straying by husband OR wife. Things are made worse as the Sheep clashes with the ruling animal of the year, the Ox. This causes misunderstandings between couples, and danger of an outsider fanning the flames from the side.

FIXING THE EXTERNAL STAR OF ROMANCE: To prevent this affliction from doing real harm to your marriage, carry the **Enhancing Relationships Amulet**, especially if you suspect your spouse already has eyes for someone outside your marriage. Or if you are constantly fighting with each other, or forced into a situation when you have to spend large amounts of time apart (e.g. if one of you commutes to a different country for work, or travel a lot for work). It is also a good idea to display a pair of **Marriage Happiness Ducks** in the SW of the home, or if

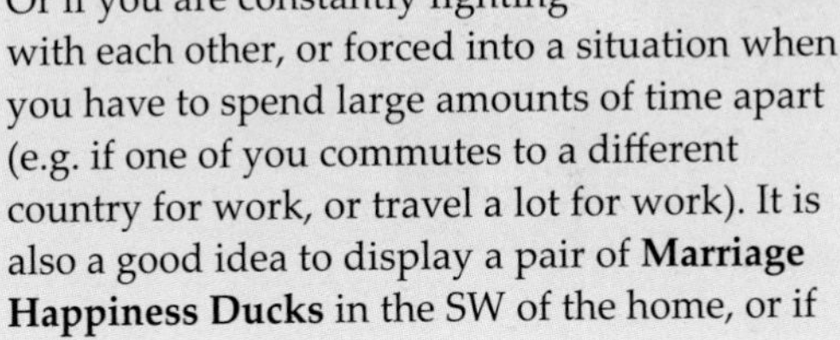

you suspect something has already started, place an **Amethyst Geode** tied with red string under the foot of the bed of the straying partner.

You can also invite in the **image of an Ox and Horse** to counter the affliction. This subdues the possibility of infidelity causing problems for you. The OX/HORSE presence will create a special "cross" with the SHEEP/RAT affliction.

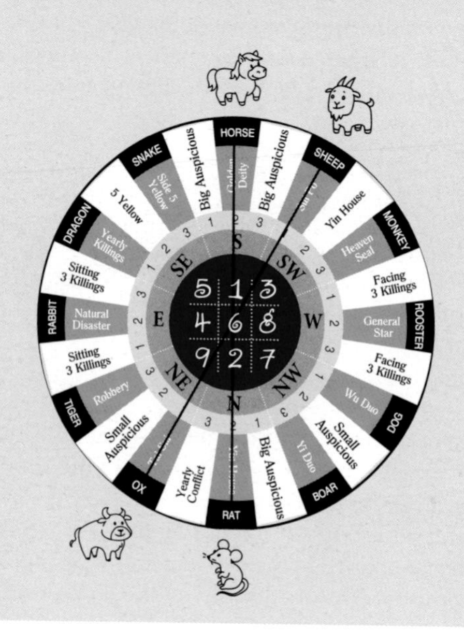

Flying Stars of 2021

Chapter 4

FLYING STAR CHART OF 2021

Heavenly Star *rules the year*

The Flying Star chart on first glance is a big improvement on last year's chart. The Loss Star #7 of 2020 makes way for the ***Heaven Star*** #6 in this Year of the Ox 2021. The Heaven Star becomes the dominant star of this year. This white star is associated with many good things, attracting the celestial luck of the heavens and providing the unseen hand of opportunity and guidance from above. Everyone stands to benefit from this star, especially if the center of the home where the star is located is kept well-energized and active throughout the year.

In 2021, it benefits to keep the center of the home very active! Have friends over & use this space well.

Rearrange your furniture so you naturally gravitate to the center of your home. The more you include this space in daily usage, the better the luck of the whole family for this coming year.

2021's chart suits homes with open plan layouts arranged around the center part of the home. This is where the luck of auspicious heaven energy congregates this year, and keeping this part of the home lively and vibrant with lots of music, chatter and activity will serve to "activate" this star, bringing it to life!

Work at repositioning your furniture and seating if you have to. This year it is extremely auspicious for all members of the household to spend plenty of time in the center sector, and when you have guests, entertain them in this part of the home. If your home has a piano, place it in the center so every time someone sits down to play it, the sector gets energized.

If your home is not an open-concept one, keep the doors to the center room in the home ajar as much as possible. You want the energy that emanates from the center to seep into all other areas of the home. The more you energize this part of your house, and the more you suppress the bad luck sectors, the better the luck of the whole household for the year.

ENHANCE THE CENTER GRID
with the Celestial Water Dragon

This year, every household benefits from the presence of the **Celestial Water Dragon**. Place this celestial creature in the center of your home and of your office. The celestial Dragon is the ultimate symbol of good fortune and its deep blue colour and cloud imagery suggest its heavenly origins. This Dragon is auspicious wherever he is displayed, but this year he especially benefits the center part of the home, which houses the Heaven Star #6.

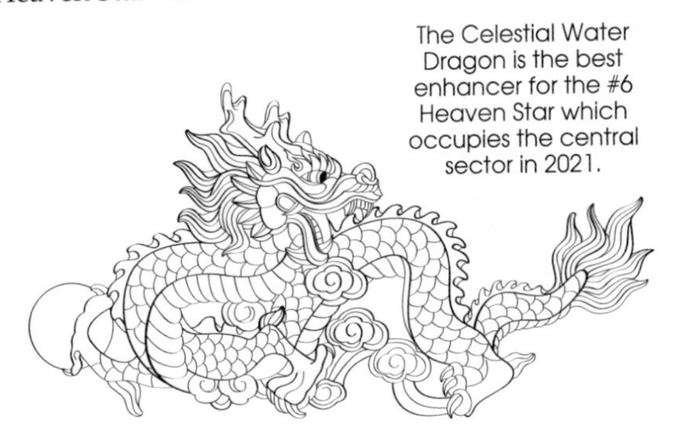

The Celestial Water Dragon is the best enhancer for the #6 Heaven Star which occupies the central sector in 2021.

Placing the celestial dragon here will attract plenty of new and lucrative opportunities into your life, as well as the patrons, mentors and contacts you need to support you in whatever path you choose to take. Individuals and organizations who are in a position to help you and to open doors for you, will somehow find their way into your life. The presence of the celestial Dragon always attracts abundance and success, and this year, inviting in this Dragon brings a very special kind of good fortune indeed.

Invoking the power of THE EIGHT IMMORTALS

Another excellent energizer for the center is the **8 Celestial Immortals Plaque**. The 8 Immortals bring eight kinds of good fortune and protects against harm. In Chinese mythology, they are a revered group of legendary beings each with a unique talent or ability. These eight saints have been depicted in Chinese art

Place the 8 Immortals Plaque in the center of the home in 2021.

since time immemorial as they are believed to bestow wealth, longevity and spiritual awakening on all who glance upon them.

Depicted as a group, they bring a balanced basket of good fortune and protection for the whole family. They hail from the 8 different compass directions and are usually shown with their unique symbols representing the luck each brings.

Zhang Guo Lao, protector of the North, **brings the luck of good descendants**. His symbol is the bamboo flute and his element is Water. He enjoys drinking wine and is famous for making his own which had curative and healing powers. He is said to be able to drink poison without harm and offers protection against the dark arts. He is often shown with his companion, the mule.

Chao Guo Jiu, protector of the Northeast, **brings the luck of control**. He is excellent for those in positions of authority who have to motivate and retain the support of those they command. His element is Earth and his symbol are the castanets. According to legend, he went to great lengths to avoid casualties of war, protecting the innocent from harm during battle. He is skilled in the magical arts and possesses great wisdom and charisma to lead with great authority.

Lee Dong Bin, protector of the West, **brings protection against evil**. His element is Metal and his implement is the Magic Sword. He is famed for being a great scholar and poet, and for his exceptional intelligence. While he had certain character flaws – he was a serial womanizer - he was known for his dedication to helping others elevate their spiritual growth.

He Xian Gu, protector of the Southwest, **bestows family and marriage luck**. Her element is Earth and her symbol is the Lotus Blossom. The only lady among the 8, she has also grown to become a symbol of woman power. She is often accompanied by a mythical bird said to reign over all birds, bringing new opportunities from near and far. She helps stabilize married couples, protecting the sacred sanctity of marriage and bestowing a happy family life. She protects against troublemakers who threaten to break up happy families. For those who are single, she is said to attract marriage opportunities and suitable suitors.

Han Xiang Zi, protector of the Southeast, **brings healing energies** to those who are sick, but more particularly, he helps heal those with a broken heart. His element is Wood and his symbol is the flute. His legendary past involves the tragic love story where he fell in love with the daughter of the Dragon King, who did not grant the couple his blessings. Theirs was a star-crossed romance without a happy ending, but the bamboo flute he wields was said to be a gift from his beloved. Playing on his flute healed him emotionally, and from there on he vowed to help others the same way.

Lan Chai He, protector of the Northwest, **brings scholastic and creative luck**. His element is Metal and his symbol the flower basket. He is often shown with his swan, symbolic of his lyrical gifts. He is said to have become immortal when the Monkey King bestowed 500 years of magic upon him. His companion is the Monkey. As well as his flair for the arts, he is said to possess a sharp intelligence and wit.

Han Zhong Li, protector of the East, **brings longevity and wealth**. His element is Wood and his symbols are the magical fan and peach. His fan is said to have the ability to heal the sick, even bring the dead back to life, as well as turning stones to silver and gold. His peach is the fruit of immortality which grants a long life filled with happiness.

Tie Guai Lee, protector of the South, **brings wisdom and healing**. His element is Fire and his symbol is the Bottle Gourd. He is often depicted as an unkempt old man with disheveled hair, taking on the appearance of a beggar. His chosen role is to care for those who are sick, poor or in need.

Enhance for Future Prosperity
in the Northeast

The animal sign of the year, the Ox plays host to the *Future Prosperity Star* #9. This star signifies imminent wealth just about to ripen, and the closer we get to Period 9, which starts Feb 4th 2024, the shorter the waiting time for what is considered "future wealth". The #9 is also a magnifying star, which gains power as we head into Period 9. The Ox sign this year thus gets energized with the presence of this star in its sector. The NE is also the place of the Tiger, who features as always in the year's Paht Chee in the month pillar.

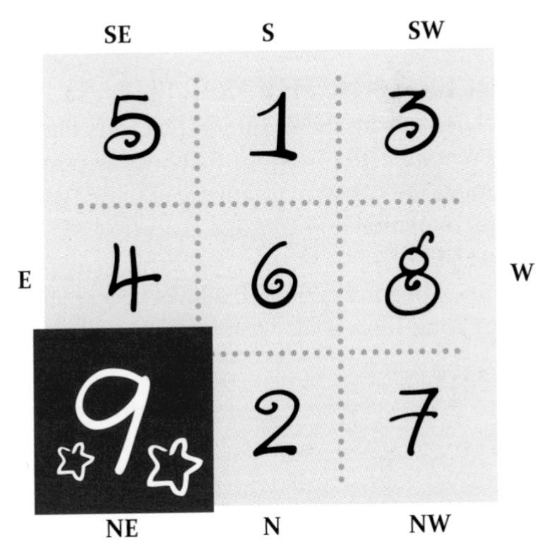

The NE plays host to the "Future Prosperity Star"

The powerful Fire star #9 brings vitality to all who come under its influence, and its presence in the ruling animal sector bodes well for the coming year. This star benefits homes that face NE, and individuals whose bedrooms or office rooms are located NE, as well as those born under the signs of Ox and Tiger.

The #9 in the NE suggests that the central #6 heavenly star gets strengthened. This is a lucky star for most of the year, except for months when monthly flying stars here are unfavourable – i.e. March, May, July, August and December 2021. When unfavourable monthly stars visit, ensure you have the relevant cures in place and keep this sector less active during these times.

ENHANCERS FOR THE NORTHEAST

The NE benefits from the **9 Golden Dragons Plaque** featuring nine celestial Dragons that bestow power and generates the capacity to pursue all one's grandest ambitions conviction and courage.

Having nine Dragons in the NE allows you to stay focused on long-term goals without getting distracted,

9 Golden Dragons Plaque

or discouraged by short-term difficulties. They protect you against those who wish to see you fail, and shields you from the effects of less ambitious relatives or acquaintances who do not have your vision.

Displaying this plaque in the NE of your home or office ensures you have the support of not one but *nine* Dragons, the number that symbolizes completion and abundance. The number 9 is a magical number as it is a number that always reduces back to itself when multiplied. It also strengthens the #9 star, which is getting stronger as we move rapidly towards a fast-approaching Period of 9.

BUILD YOUR WEALTH: You should also activate the NE with a collection of **Wealth Cabinets**. These wealth cabinets symbolize an accumulation of asset wealth, meaning that the money you make accrues into ever-larger amounts that can last into the many generations. Energizing the NE helps you to make enough money so you do not have to spend everything you earn. It allows you to grow wealthy enough to carve out a secure, comfortable and worry-free future for yourself and your loved ones.

Activate for Love & Romance
in the EAST

The Peach Blossom Star #4 settles into in the East sector this year. This star gets greatly enhanced in 2021 as the East is the place of the Rabbit, the creature associated with the Moon, and with the Goddess of the Moon who governs all fortunes to do with love, romance and relationships. Legend has it that when you catch the attention of the Moon Goddess, she aids you in all matters related to the heart, improving relations between lovers and even matchmaking those who are destined to be together.

The East plays host to the Peach Blossom Star, which brings romance.

For those who are single, activating this sector with the **Rabbit in the Moon** awakens the powers of **Moon Goddess**, alerting her to all wishes to do with affairs of the heart. Enhancing this sector promotes the success of relationships, attracts marriage opportunities, smooths interactions between spouses, and imbues stale marriages with a newfound passion and vigour.

The EAST becomes the place of the MOON RABBIT in 2021, harnessing the power of the Lunar Mansions to bring great love and romance into the lives of those who activate this luck.

This is the sector to enhance if love is what you are looking for! This year we have designed the **Rabbit in the Moon**, the earthly messenger of this lunar goddess. Placing this activator in the East will help singles meet their soulmates and forever partners, while helping those who are already married to keep their spouses. Remember that this year's Paht Chee generates the unfavourable *External Flower of Romance Star*, which can cause problems within already existing relationships, resulting in unwanted love triangles and other outside disturbances to a love relationship. Invoking the blessings of the **Rabbit in the Moon** ensures that only the positive aspects of love materialize. It will also protect against unpleasantness associated with matters of the heart. They say there is nothing sweeter than love, but they also say that nothing breaks like a heart – remember the song by Mark Ronson and Miley Cyrus? Heartache and heartbreak can be far more painful than physical pain; the #4 in the East brings the Moon Rabbit to life and provides a solution for those looking for happiness in love.

ATTRACTING MARRIAGE OPPORTUNITIES

For those looking for a soul mate, someone you can settle down with and make a future with, or if you are already dating but your partner seems a long way off from proposing marriage, you can speed things along with the help of your **Peach Blossom Animal**. Our new Peach Blossom animals the **Rat**, **Rabbit**, **Horse** and **Rooster** come with trees of fortune enhanced with potent symbols of love and marriage.

The **Peach Blossom Rabbit** brings love and marriage opportunities to the **Dog**, **Tiger** and **Horse**. If you are a Dog looking for love that leads to marriage, or you would like your current partner to propose, display a **Peach Blossom Rabbit** in the WEST, or in the EAST in 2021.

Peach Blossom Rabbit

For students,
activate the Scholastic Star in the EAST

For young people and anyone pursuing their studies, engaged in research or in search of new knowledge, they can activate the scholastic star of the year which flies to the East in 2021. The #4 is also the star number that brings study and exam luck; when properly activated, it has the power to help you achieve success in anything related to scholastic accolades. Enhancing this star improves clarity of mind, allowing you to absorb new knowledge and to process it with much greater efficiency. Anything requiring cognitive

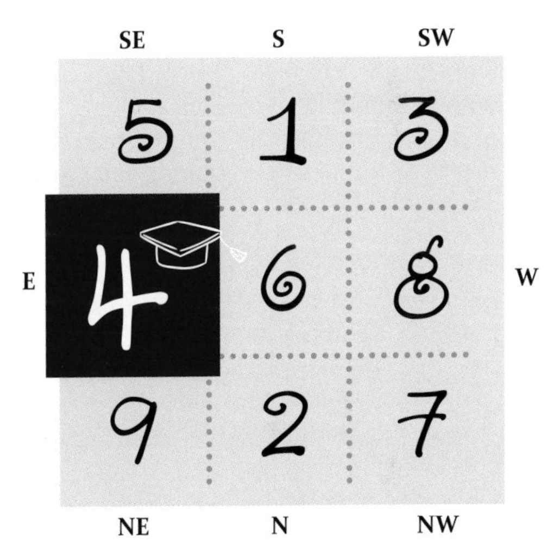

The #4 star in the East is also the Star of Scholarship

reasoning and abilities gets enhanced when you harness the energies of this star number.

The #4 Scholastic Star also boosts creativity and original thinking, allowing you to better come up with unique and innovative new ideas. This star gets strengthened this year, as it is a Wood star flying into a Wood sector.

ENHANCE THE SCHOLASTIC STAR:
The best way to activate the #4 for scholastic luck is to carry **Manjushri's Gau**. Manjushri is the Buddha of Wisdom, and when you call on his help, he slices through your ignorance so only wisdom remains. His flaming sword removes all that is obscured in your mind, allowing you to think with a clear head so you can map out effective solutions to everything you are pursuing.

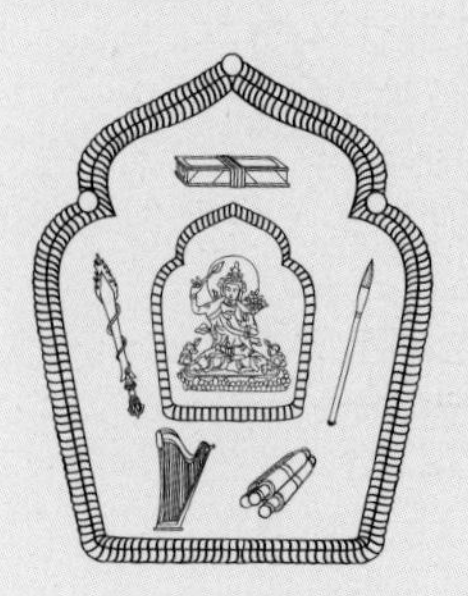

For students taking exams, having Manjushri's support enables them to recall everything they have revised and studied, and to write excellent answers in their exam. Manjushri boosts everything to do with wisdom and intelligence, and helps one to make wise choices. He ensures one constantly sees the big picture, while also filling in the details. For school-going children, they can clip **Manjushri's Amulet** onto their schoolbag. The specially-designed **Scholastic Amulet with Manjushri's mantra** sums up all of his wisdom and blessings, providing an endless stream of support, reinforcement and inspiration.

FOR EXAM LUCK:

For students taking important exams and hoping to do well, there is no better enhancer than the **Dragon Carp**. The carp that jumps over the Dragon Gate and successfully transforms into a Dragon is the best symbol of success for anyone aspiring to scholastic success. It promotes the luck of the scholarship and helps students not just pass exams but excel in them. The Dragon Carp also generates a strong sense of self-motivation, ensuring one does not fall into bad company or get side-tracked into unproductive tasks. This is the best enhancer for children or teenagers looking to perform well in important exams, to win awards, to gain scholarships and grants and to gain admission into colleges of their choice.

The academic path of today is filled with potholes and pitfalls, as everything has become more competitive. More and more people are fighting for fewer places at the top universities; at school, children are faced with stiff competition with Tiger parents in the sidelines egging them on. For a young mind, it can all become too much, and with all the expectations heaped on young shoulders these days, sometimes all it takes is one bad test or one bad result to cause a child to throw in the towel and just give up.

As parents, we need to imbue in our children not just the impetus to keep striving for the top, but help them understand there will be bumps and disappointments along the way. It is not necessary to perform every single day of the year, to come out top in every single test; what is important is to peak when it counts. The **Dragon Carp** stabilizes one's mind, helping a child along the academic path and to navigate all that comes his or her way with a strong and mature mind, resulting in success when it truly matters.

Transform Five Yellow Misfortune Star *in the Southeast*

The bogus star, the Five Yellow, makes its way into the Southeast this year. The good news is that because the Southeast is a Wood Sector, it mitigates the extent of damage of this dangerous Earth star, as Wood destroys Earth in the cycle of elements. When the Five Yellow flies into a Wood sector, misfortune can be turned into opportunity. This is why we have designed this year's **Five Element Pagoda with a Tree of Life**. This alters the effects of the *wu wang*, suppressing the darker side of this star while

The 5 Yellow afflicts the SE in 2021 but with the correct cure, this Five Yellow has the potential to bring great good luck!

harnessing its benevolent powers. This star affects those living in homes that face SE, those with bedrooms or work rooms in the SE, and those born in years of the Dragon and Snake.

If your house has more than one level, make sure you have a **Five Element Pagoda with Tree of Life** on every floor. Keep the SE of the home free from too much activity and noise, and avoid renovations in this part of the home in 2021. Whatever you do, DO NOT renovate the SE of the home this year.

Victory Star brings winning luck *to the South*

The White Star #1 associated with victory and winning luck makes its way to the South. This star allows you to triumph in any situation and to attain success over any competition you may face. In 2021, this star benefits those whose bedrooms are located South, and all those living in homes that face South. Anyone who spends a lot of time in this part of their home can also tap into the good luck this star brings by keeping it well energized with the correct activators. The livelier you keep this part of the home, the better!

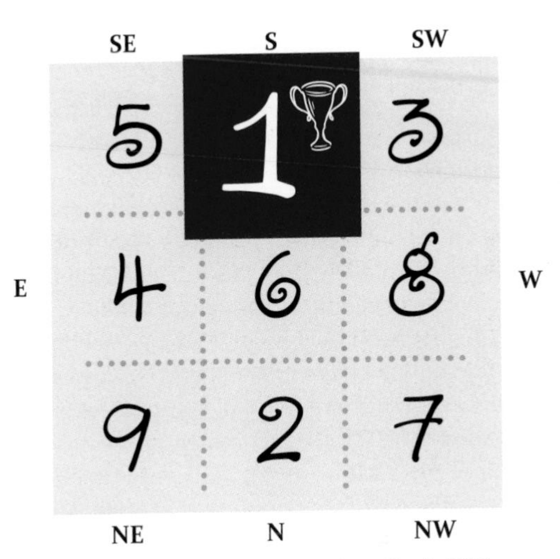

The South sector enjoys the Victory Star in 2021.

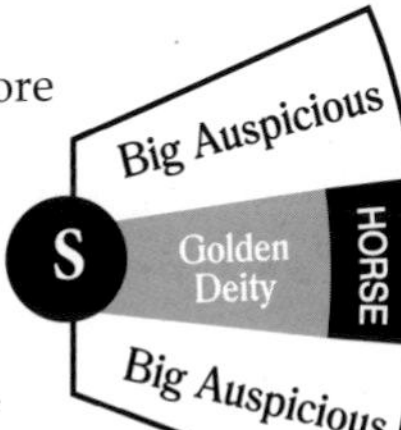

The Victory Star this year is made more potent as it is supported by not one but **TWO Big Auspicious Stars** from the 24 Mountains, as well as the **Golden Deity Star**, echoing the benefits of the ruling star of the year, the #6 Heaven Star. All this serves to increase the power and effectiveness of this star, so it is really worthwhile to actively enhance this star. Because the South is the sector governing the reputation of the household, the #1 here also improves one's standing and repute in various circles – work, social, etc.

ACTIVATE THE VICTORY STAR:
The best enhancer for the Victory Star is the **Victorious Windhorse Carrying a Jewel**. The Windhorse is the very essence of success luck, known as the magical steed of the folk hero King Gesar, who when riding his Windhorse could never be defeated. His horse with flaming red coat has become synonymous with success and victory, and his image is what is needed whenever one needs to boost one's chances against others in any kind of competitive situation. In 2021, we recommend for everyone to place the Victorious Windhorse in the South. This sector is also the home sector of the Horse, an auspicious creature that emanates pure Fire energy. Displaying images and figurines of horses in the South is thus very appropriate and auspicious indeed.

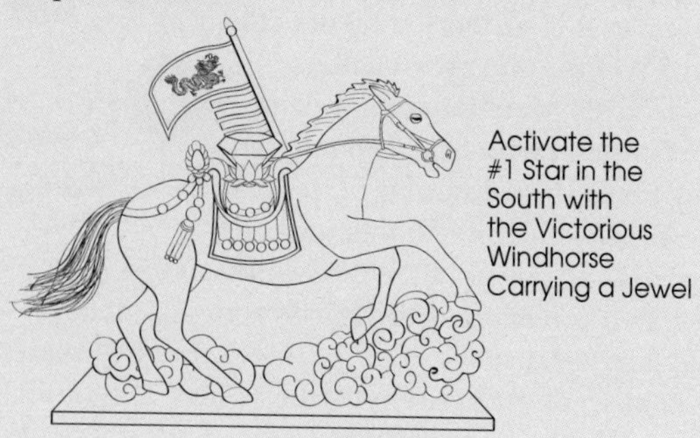

Activate the #1 Star in the South with the Victorious Windhorse Carrying a Jewel

BOOST POWER AND AUTHORITY:
For those in positions of leadership and management, the best way to enhance your effectiveness as a leader is with the help of the **Ru Yi**. The Ru Yi is the royal scepter of power, which bestows "the right to rule". In ancient China, anyone in any kind of power would never be seen without a Ru Yi at his side. You can place your Ru Yi in front of you on your work desk, or carry in your bag.

The **Crimson Red Ru Yi with Bats** brings the luck of **success and abundance**. Any boss, head or leader can use the help of this Ru Yi to ensure things between all in their group stay harmonious, joyful and productive at all times. It attracts the luck of abundance and success, so whatever is pursued turns out fruitful and effective. It helps you to ensure all your final goals are reached in the most harmonious way.

Anyone in any kind of leadership position needs a Ru Yi.

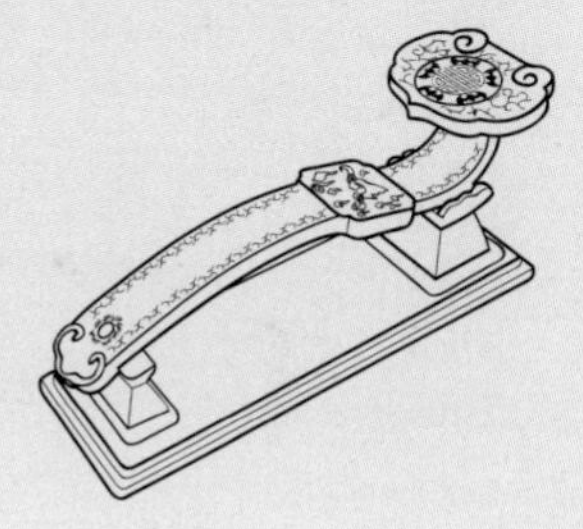

The **Deep Blue Ru Yi with 8 Auspicious Symbols** brings the luck of **wealth**. This Ru Yi includes the Victory Banner for winning luck, the Double Fish for abundance, the Parasol for protection, the Conch for good news, the Wheel for sustainability, the Mystic Knot for longevity, the Vase for completion and the Lotus for good intentions.

These symbols of good fortune are the magical implements of the Eight Immortals, and act as vessels of their power. Carrying images of their magical symbols on a Ru Yi imbues you with a complete collection of the different kinds of luck you need to reach your full potential as a leader.

The **Yellow Ru Yi with Celestial Dragon** brings the luck of **power and position.** Those operating in political environments or in politics need this Ru Yi! It bestows charisma and magnetism, and endows strength to make your position one that is stable and secure. It ensures you do not get plotted against and overthrown. It protects against betrayal and treachery and gives you power over those on the outside as well as on the inside.

The SOUTH is the place to activate if success, victory, fame and reputation is what you seek.

Suppress the Quarrelsome Star *in the Southwest*

The Quarrelsome Star #3 flies to the Southwest, bringing hostile energy and complications associated with arguments, misunderstandings and court cases. The #3 star can also cause serious aggravations that lead to violence and tragedy. This affliction affects anyone with a bedroom in the SW, those whose main doors face SW, and those born in years of the Sheep and Monkey. It also affects the Matriarch of the household. The #3 star is especially strong this year,

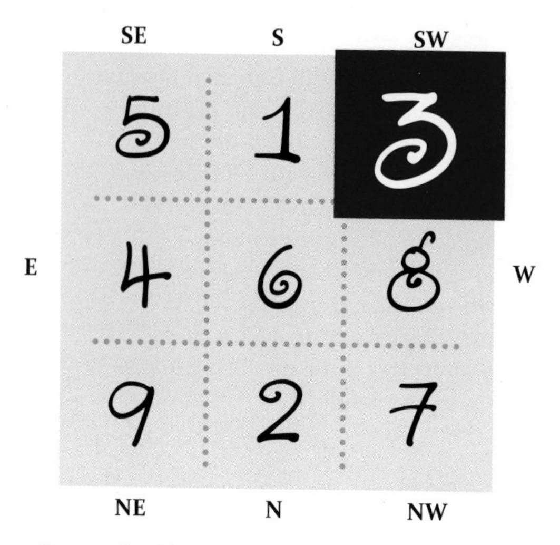

Beware the #3 quarrelsome star in the SW this year.

as the intrinsic Wood energy of the star dominates the Earth energy of the SW. The effects of this star are made worse as the SW also plays host to the **Yin House** from the 24 Mountains. All this suggests that this affliction MUST be taken seriously.

Anything that suggests Fire is an effective cure, so keeping the lights turned on brightly in this sector will help combat the negative energies of this star. **The colour red** is also suitable, so red curtains, rugs and cushion covers here will help very much indeed.

CURES FOR THE QUARRELSOME STAR:
For 2021, the best remedy for the Quarrelsome Star in the SW is the **Nine Phoenix Plaque** in red and gold. These celestial birds in red and gold - which represent the elements of Fire and Metal - work to subdue this troublesome Wood Star. The Fire energy engulfs the Wood of the #3, while the Metal energy of the gold effectively subdues it.

The Nine Phoenix Plaque is an excellent cure against the #3 Quarrelsome Star.

We also recommend placing **red carpets** in this sector, or in the SW portion of any room you spend a lot of time in. Another effective cure for the #3 are the **Red Peace and Harmony Apples**. In Chinese, the word for peaceful is *Ping,* which sounds like the word for apple – *Ping Kor*. This year's Peace Apples comes embossed with the English word "Peace" and the Chinese rhyming couplet carrying the meaning "If your intentions are good and your heart is pure, the world will be peaceful."

Place this pair of apples in the SW to ensure all members of the household stay supportive of one another, and to prevent clashes and conflict from arising. Also an excellent cure for use within the office to maintain a productive and supportive environment between colleagues and workmates.

Enhance Prosperity Star 8 *in the West*

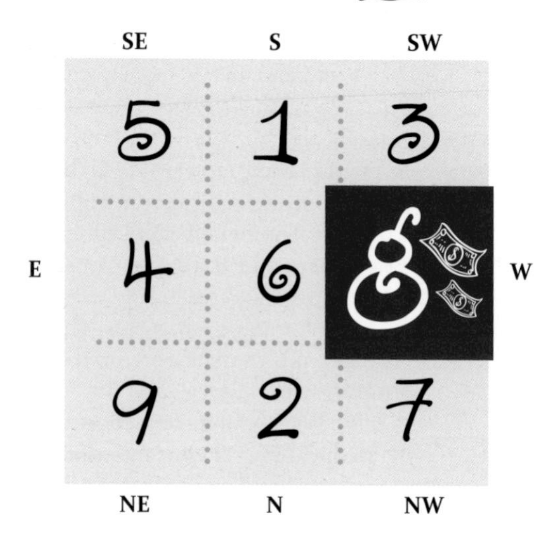

The Wealth Star #8 flies to the West this year.

The very lucky Wealth Star #8 makes its way to the West, the sector of the Rooster. This star is also known as the *Current Prosperity Star*, as we are currently in the Period of 8. The West is the sector that represents children and descendants, suggesting that the wealth this sector brings will last into the long term, reaching future generations and for many generations to come. It points to a successful accumulation of assets over time if properly energized.

In 2021, the West can be considered one of the luckiest areas of the home, because it enjoys this auspicious #8 star. The strong energy of the current period emanating from this sector benefits all homes whose main entrances face West, and all bedrooms and offices located in the West benefit from this luck. The West is also the place of the youngest daughter, so the wealth this sector brings benefits the young girls of the house.

WEALTH luck takes root in the WEST sector this year, so this is the area of the home you should enhance for greater prosperity luck.

Remember that to activate the luck of this auspicious star #8, the West should be thoroughly imbued with yang energy - this means lots of activity, lots of noise and plenty of bright lights. When there is movement, sound, chatter and merry-making, the number 8 comes to life, bringing good fortune and big prosperity. In the constellations, 8 is a "man-made star" with two assistants – on the right and on the left - so that at its strongest moments, it brings wealth and great nobility.

When the 8 can turn dangerous...

Beware however. The number becomes negative when afflicted by structures in the environment that threaten its location. If the West sector of your home has too much Metal energy, or if there are harmful physical structures that cause poison arrows to direct threatening energy your way, that is when the number 8 can bring harm to young children especially young daughters of the household, causing illness to arise. If there are such structures external to your home, but towards the West, it is important to block the view with curtains, or dissipate the killing energy with **facetted crystal balls**. These will disperse the worst of the killing breath before it has the chance to enter your home.

If the view from your window to the WEST is of a threatening looking building with sharp edges or poison arrows, keep the curtains in this area closed to block the offending view from spoiling your feng shui. Hang facetted crystal balls here.

ACTIVATE FOR WEALTH IN THE WEST

The best way to manifest wealth luck in 2021 is the make sure the West part of your home is well-energized with wealth symbols. Because this is the year of the Ox, this creature is especially lucky as it symbolizes harnessing the good fortune of the year. Because the West represents children and descendants, this prosperity luck benefits the whole family not just in the present but into the long term.

The image of the Ox has great power to attract abundant good fortune in 2021. Displaying images of the Ox in all sizes and permutations is so lucky this year! For the collectors among you, a good time to start "collecting" Ox images.

A fabulous wealth enhancer for this year is the **Asset Wealth Bull**. This Bull holds the symbolic and subliminal message "May the market bull for you"! With resplendent red saddle and surrounded by coins, ingots and symbols of prosperity, this bull energizes for wealth of the kind that can accumulate into expanded net worth, the kind that provides meaningful disposable income, providing a worry-free future.

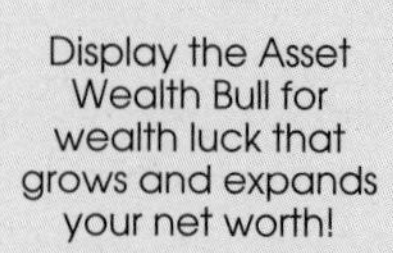
Display the Asset Wealth Bull for wealth luck that grows and expands your net worth!

To tap the hidden wealth of the year, display the **Ox finding Hidden Wealth**. This Ox is depicting calmly and unobtrusively grazing in a field full of coins, sniffing out hidden wealth and opportunities. In a year with little obvious wealth but a lot of hidden wealth, this Ox generates the luck that allows you to tap the full potential of the year.

Invite in the "Ox Finding Hidden Wealth" to tap the full potential of the year.

Another great activator for this year's wealth star is the **Tree Bringing 3 Kinds of Wealth**.

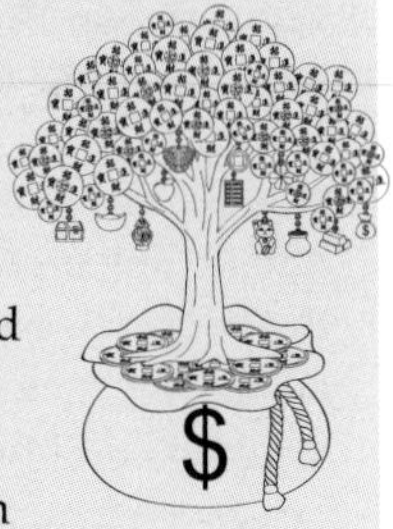

Trees always depict growth energy, and when they look like money trees, they really do bring the luck of wealth into the home! Our tree this year has been designed to represent the manifestation of 3 different kinds of wealth - Asset Wealth, Income Wealth and Growth Wealth. Having all three kinds of wealth brings you not just enough to lead a comfortable life now, it gives you security and peace of mind and allows you to plan for the future. This year's wealth tree also features 12 lucky charms to signify abundance in all forms entering your life - the Double Fish, the Apple, the Treasure Chest, the Golden Ingot, the Wealth Vase, the Abacus, the I-Ching Coin, Gold bars, the 4-leafed clover the Maneki Neko Lucky Cat and the Pot of Gold.

This year's wealth tree represents not just prosperity luck but also the luck of asset accumulation. This symbolises your wealth growing and your networth expanding.

Beware Betrayal & Loss Star
in the Northwest

A dangerous aspect of this year's chart is the #7 Robbery Star in the NW. This brings loss and betrayal energies to the Patriarch, which not only means the patriarch of the family, but leaders, bosses, managers and anyone responsible for the welfare or livelihood of others. The presence of the #7 in the NW suggests that the Patriarch could get cheated, conned or betrayed. It brings the energy that suggests you should keep your friends close but your enemies closer.

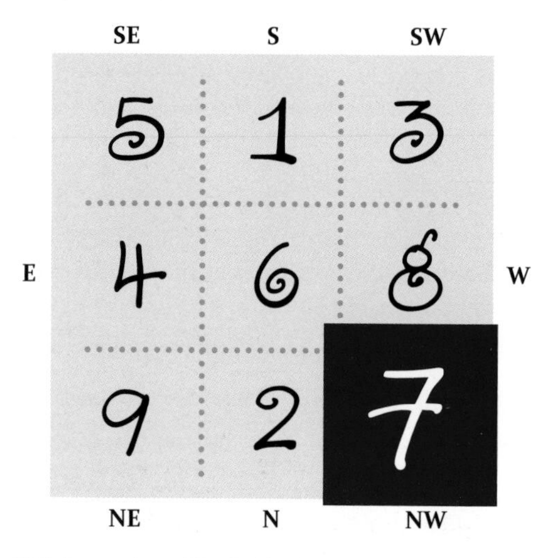

The NW, the sector of the Patriarch and Leader, gets afflicted by the #7 Loss and Betrayal Star in 2021.

In 2021, keep your friends close but your enemies closer!

Stay alert like a hawk, as treachery can strike at any moment. The energies of the year could corrupt even the most trustworthy of friends and the most loyal of employees. The #7 Robbery Star, like its namesake, describes a situation when you are cheated out of money; but it can also manifest as an actual robbery. We recommend all who stay out late, or who venture anywhere even remotely unsafe, to carry the **Nightspot Protection Amulet**. Because this star affects the NW, it harms the Father the most, but there can be knock-on adverse effects on the rest of the family, or the rest of a leader's charges.

CURE FOR #7 STAR: This year the best cure for the #7 star in the home is the **Anti-Burglary Plaque with Door Guardians.** These Door Gods with spear in the ready are depicted with the Anti-Burglary Amulets, with the Chinese proverb, "May your family be blessed with peace, safety and abundant joy, may your home be filled with everlasting happiness."

Display in the NW to ensure your home stays protected against unexpected and unwanted intruders, who may cause not just loss of property and possessions, but loss of peace of mind. These door guardians will help keep your family protected through the year.

BEWARE BETRAYAL:

This year, risk of betrayal is rife as the #7 star occupies the NW, the location of the leader. Betrayal means duplicity from those you trust, those you least suspect and therefore those you are most vulnerable to. While it feels nasty to get cheated by conmen and people you do not know, when betrayals come from those closest to you, the harm is emotional as well as physical. The loss is no longer merely monetary, it hits a nerve deep within that can be difficult to take and recover from. This year, because opportunity for this to happen gets increased, we suggest to remove temptation where you can, watch your back, and carry symbols to protect against this kind of bad luck. Carry the **Kuan Kung Anti-Betrayal Amulet**. This specially-designed talisman features the amulet that protects against being stabbed in the back, with the mantra that ensures the protection is effective.

PROTECT AGAINST BEING CHEATED:
For those engaging in high-risk deals carry the **Anti-Cheating Amulet** to ensure you do not get conned by unscrupulous people. An excellent amulet for business people and for anyone dealing with new acquaintances who maybe be untrustworthy.

PROTECTION AGAINST THE DARK ARTS:
Another form of harm can come from those who practice black magic. Especially in the East, such arts are more common than you think. Even if you do not subscribe or "believe" in this kind of power, it exists. Someone who projects negative thoughts against you, whether out of spite, jealousy or some other reason, does not even have to be skilled in these methods to send negative hexes and projectiles your way!

For example, if someone curses you on the street because they are angry at the way you drive, this can result in the same kind of misfortune effect as someone actively plotting or using black magic against you. The latter is of course more serious, but whenever one is weak in terms of spirit essence and element luck, they can succumb badly when someone forms negative thoughts and sends those thoughts their way.

The best protection against this kind of harm is the **28 Hums Protection Wheel**, which features the powerful **Heart Sutra** on the back. These sacred syllables together with this powerful sutra ensures that whatever projectiles are sent your way cannot reach you. A vital cure for anyone with enemies, who are engaged in high stakes deals, or anyone who may have offended someone intentionally or unintentionally.

28 Hums Protection Wheel

Suppress Illness Star
in the North

The #2 Illness Star flies to the North, and because North is of the Water element, it cannot do anything on its own to weaken the energies of the #2, an Earth star. The Illness Star is further strengthened as it is supported by the **Yin House Star** in North 2, the sector of the Rat. This boosts the potency of this star, making the North sector dangerous for those who are elderly, frail or prone to illness.

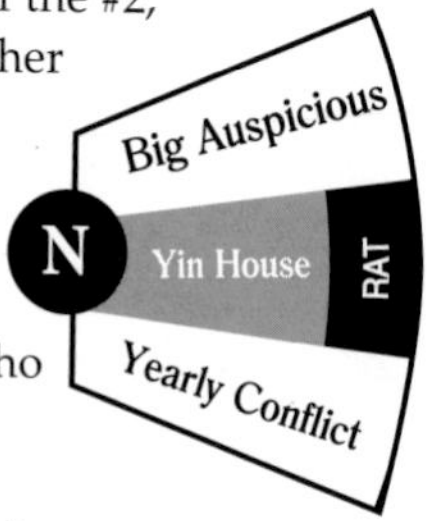

Big Auspicious
N
Yin House
RAT
Yearly Conflict

It is important for anyone whose bedroom is facing North, or whose home faces North to suppress the Illness Star with strong cures.

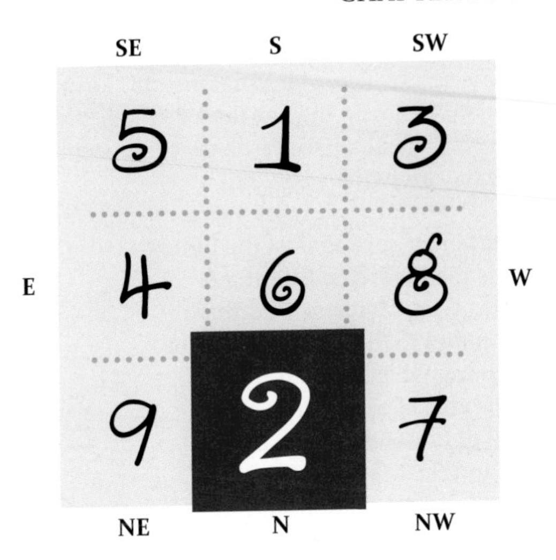

The North gets afflicted by the Illness Star this year.

CURE FOR THE ILLNESS STAR:

In 2021, a good cure for the Illness Star is the **Healing Deer Carrying Vase of Longevity with Linzhi**. The deer is renowned by the Chinese for their powerful curative properties and is often seen as the companion of the God of Longevity, Sau Seng Kong. With the world caught up in fears of epidemics and pandemics where there seems no escape with a proper cure a long time coming, the deer is an excellent shield against this kind of illness. Display in the North of the home this year. The Healing Deer is an excellent symbol of good health in the year 2021.

Another potent cure against the Illness Star #2 is the **Medicine Buddha & 7 Sugatas Gau**. Medicine Buddha always comes to the aid of those who are suffering when one calls for his help. His area of expertise is in the removal of poisons, disease and illness, and the **Medicine Buddha & 7 Sugatas Gau** features all 8 of his emanations, and his powerful mantras in whole. You can place in the North of the home to stay under his protection constantly. Excellent for anyone who is ill or feeling unwell.

You can also chant his mantra daily:
TADYATHA OM BHEKHANDZYE BHEKHANDZYE MAHA BHEKHANDZYE (BHEKHANDZYE) RADZA SAMUGATE SOHA

For those suffering from a chronic ailment, we suggest that you get yourself a dedicated **Medicine Buddha Mala** to chant with. The more you chant his mantra over the mala, the more powerful the mala will become. Keep the mala with you always, and whenever you have spare time, bring it out and chant. You can also wear the mala as an accessory around your wrist or neck.

AGAINST COVID-19: To protect against the coronavirus specifically, the best cure is to invite in an image of the **Buddha Vairocana**, who brings blessings of good health but also provides strong protection against contagious diseases. Display his image as a figurine, and also carry his image in the form of a **Gold Talisman Card** which we have made available to help tide us through these challenging times.

AFFLICTIONS OF 2021
TAI SUI *in the NORTHEAST*

The TAI SUI or God of the Year always occupies the sector of the ruling animal sign of the year. This year, he occupies the palace of the Ox, Northeast 1. The Tai Sui is the celestial force that governs all that happens on Earth, and when one has his support and blessings, very little can go wrong, but when one offends him, his wrath knows no bounds.

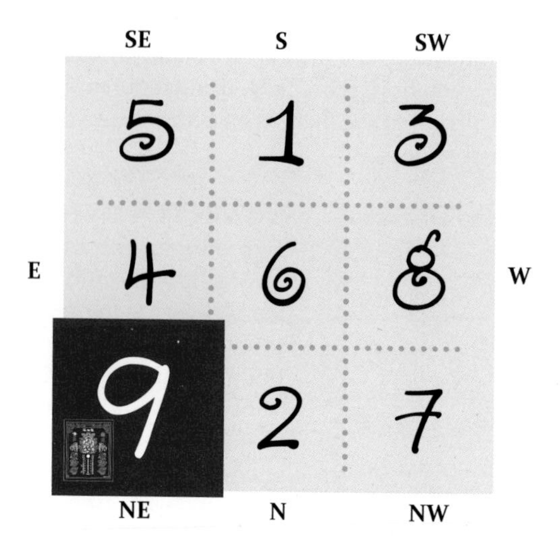

It is a matter of course and tradition for most Chinese who believe, to offer prayers to Tai Sui at the start of the year, humbly asking for his help and support for the coming year. In feng shui, the creature that is known to appease him is the celestial chimera the **Dragon Pi Xie**, so we always recommend to place this in the location of the Tai Sui.

The Dragon Pi Xie is said to appease the Tai Sui. Place in the NE in 2021.

PROTECTION: What is even more important is to place the **Tai Sui Plaque** with his image and invocation as a sign of respect. In 2021, place this in the NE1 sector. Animal signs especially affected by the Tai Sui this year are the Earth signs of Sheep, Dragon and Dog, while the Ox whose location he occupies should also be mindful of his presence there. For these 4 signs, we also recommend carrying the **Tai Sui Amulet** at all times throughout the year.

THREE KILLINGS in the EAST

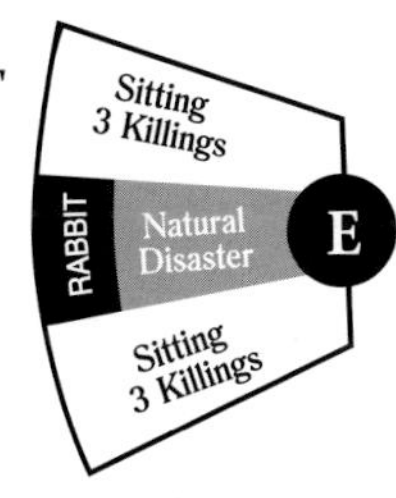

This affliction is said to bring three types of misfortune – loss of wealth, loss of reputation and loss of a loved one. All three are devastating, and when not one but three forms of bad luck hit you at once, the loss can be difficult and extremely distressing. This is another affliction that is important to take note of and to cure.

Firstly, NEVER have your back to the Three Killings affliction, so in 2021, DO NOT SIT FACING WEST,

EVEN if WEST is your best direction! Do not sit with your back to the East, as the Three Killings is the kind of affliction that stabs you in the back, when you are least suspecting. It carries the characteristic of hitting you when you are most comfortable and least aware. When things are at their calmest, beware, because the storm is about to pound and crash down...

NEVER HAVE YOUR BACK TO THE EAST this year! Make sure you do not get stabbed by the dangerous 3 Killings affliction!

CURE FOR THE THREE KILLINGS: Place the **3 Celestial Shields** to combat the Three Killings. These shields act as effective armour sheltering you from the effects of this difficult affliction. All homes should display these shields in the EAST of the home in 2021. Anyone with something to lose, who operate where stakes are high, or who are going through years of low element luck are also recommended to carry the **3 Celestial Shields Amulet** when on the go. Use as a keychain or bag decoration.

Compatibilities with other Signs in 2021

Chapter 5

The Dog in 2021 needs to try harder for relationships to work out

The Dog has to battle through the coming year afflicted by the Betrayal Star. This will affect your relationships, not just because of risk of betrayal from others but because you yourself feel more wary and suspicious. Romance is far from your mind unless someone you can really connect with enters the picture. The reality however is that when you go through a year like this one, you need the support of friends and loved ones more than ever. Making more of an effort to be agreeable will help you improve all your relationships. And if you are serious about finding love, be more proactive!

Many different influences come into play each year to determine how one animal sign gets along with another. Chinese astrology has so many permutations that it is difficult to take note of everything, but examining some of the main variables can give useful insights to the general mood and compatibility between any two signs in any year. The annual energies of the year have a larger bearing on the effect on your relationships than you may be aware of, and understanding these effects allows you to be more effective in all your interactions.

When you find the keys to unlock what makes your connections tick, not only this help with your happiness levels, it also improves your productivity and success potential.

Every animal sign under the Chinese Zodiac system has certain signs they are naturally drawn towards; certain signs make better spouses, others make more exciting lovers, others still work better when you remain platonic friends. Certain pairings thrive in a business relationship, as boss and employee, mentor and mentee; others work well as parent and child, siblings, sporting teammates or drinking buddies; while others still, have the potential to change your life in a big way.

There are also certain signs you need to stay alert to and be wary of. One's Zodiac Adversary is the animal sign born six years apart from you, the sign directly opposite you in the Zodiac wheel – but in certain years, your "natural enemy" can become a useful ally, while in others, you would be best advised to stay well clear of each other. Having knowledge of how the year's energies influence your relationships will give you the edge when it comes to how you relate to others in any given year.

In this section, we analyse the relationship between the Dog and the other signs of the Zodiac, looking in particular at the quality and nature of the relationships as determined by the influences of 2021.

1. Alliance of Allies

There are four affinity groupings that form natural allies in the horoscope. The three signs in each group have similar thought processes, aspirations and goals. Their attitudes are alike, and their support of each other is immediate and instinctive. If there is an alliance within a family unit amongst siblings, or between spouses and their child, the family is incredibly supportive, giving strength to each other. In good years, auspicious luck gets multiplied.

Astrological allies always get along. Any falling out is temporary. They trust each other and close ranks against external threats. Good astrological feng shui

ALLY GROUPINGS	ANIMALS	CHARACTERISTICS
Competitors	Rat, Dragon, Monkey	Competent, Tough, Resolute
Intellectuals	Ox, Snake, Rooster	Generous, Focused, Resilient
Enthusiasts	Dog, Tiger, Horse	Aggressive, Rebellious, Coy
Diplomats	Boar, Sheep, Rabbit	Creative, Kind, Emotional

comes from carrying the image of your allies, especially when they are going through good years.

When all three signs in a particular year has good fortune, the alliance is strengthened. But in years when one sign stands out with superior luck, the others in its grouping can "lean" on that sign to lift itself up. The Dog belongs to the grouping of Intellectuals in the Zodiac, comprising the Dog, Tiger and Horse.

This year, the strongest link in the Dog's alliance of allies is the Tiger, who has the most promising element luck in the group. For the Dog, friends born in the year of the Tiger become a very good influence on you and brings you good fortune luck.

In 2021, the Dog can lean on the Tiger to gain strength. It favours the Dog to fraternize with friends born in the year of the Tiger. The excellent element luck of your ally the Tiger gives you a boost of confidence and a line to significant contacts and opportunities.

If you do not have close friends born in a Tiger year, you can simulate this luck with the image of the Tiger. Wearing **Tiger amulets** or displaying the Tiger in your living space brings you much good fortune luck this year. Because the Tiger is closely related to many Wealth Gods from the Chinese pantheon of Deities, displaying Tigers accompanying these Wealth Deities brings not just relationship luck to the Dog, but wealth luck as well.

The Dog benefits from the presence of the Tiger in 2021. This is your astrological ally enjoying superlative element luck, and keeping a Tiger image close allows you to "borrow" some of this luck.

2. Zodiac Soulmates

Another natural ally for you is your Zodiac soulmate. In Chinese astrology, there are six pairs of signs that create six Zodiac Houses of yin and yang soulmates. Each pair creates powerful bonding on a cosmic level. Marriages or business unions between people belonging to the same Zodiac House are extremely auspicious. In a marriage, there is great love and devotion, and in a commercial partnership, it promises much wealth and success. Such a pairing is also good between professional colleagues or between siblings.

The strength of each pair is different, each having a defining strength with some making better commercial than marriage partners. How successful you are as a pair depends on how you bond. The table on the following page summarizes the key strength of each Zodiac house.

For the Dog, your Zodiac Soulmate is the Boar. Together you form the *House of Domesticity*. This is a wonderful alliance that as a team generates beautiful family harmony because these are two animal signs for whom domestic bliss is more important than anything else. Family is extremely important to you both, so the bond you share is strong and powerfully loyal. A marriage between the two of you is certain to be harmonious and happy.

In 2021 however, both Dog and Boar are not feeling particularly upbeat, but despite difficulties this year, you

HOUSES OF PAIRED SOULMATES

ANIMALS	YIN/ YANG	ZODIAC HOUSE	TARGET UNLEASHED
Rat & Ox	YANG /YIN	***House of Creativity & Cleverness***	The Rat initiates The Ox completes
Tiger & Rabbit	YANG /YIN	***House of Growth & Development***	The Tiger uses strength The Rabbit uses negotiation
Dragon & Snake	YANG /YIN	***House of Magic & Spirituality***	The Dragon takes action The Snake creates magic
Horse & Sheep	YANG /YIN	***House of Passion & Sexuality***	The Horse embodies strength & courage The Sheep embodies seduction & allure
Monkey & Rooster	YANG /YIN	***House of Career & Commerce***	The Monkey creates good strategy The Rooster takes timely action
Dog & Boar	YANG /YIN	***House of Domesticity***	The Dog creates alliances The Boar benefits

should work through any issues, as in the long run, this pairing is extremely beneficial for you both. Should you be in a commercial arrangement with one another, it benefits Dog to trust the Boar to get the job done. This is not a year for the Dog to be too active in business.

3. Secret Friends

Another extremely powerful affinity arises when two secret friends come together. There are six pairs of secret friends in the Zodiac. Love, respect and goodwill flow freely between you. Once forged, your bond is extremely hard to break. Even when you yourselves want to break it, it will be hard for either party to walk away. This pair of signs will stick together through thick and thin.

The Dog's secret friend is the Rabbit. There is a bond between these two signs despite their different

PAIRINGS OF SECRET FRIENDS	
Rat	Ox
Boar	Tiger
Dog	Rabbit
Dragon	Rooster
Snake	Monkey
Horse	Sheep

personalities. These two are soulmates always on the side of the other. A marriage between them promises much happiness, as both are amiable individuals for whom giving in will never be a problem. This year the Rabbit has better luck potential than the Dog, but with a Rabbit partner, Dog benefits.

4. Peach Blossom Links

Each alliance of allies has a special relationship with one of the four primary signs of Horse, Rat, Rooster and Rabbit in that these are the symbolic representations of love and romance for one alliance group of animal signs. These are referred to as *Peach Blossom Animals,* and the presence of their images in the homes of the matching alliance of allies brings peach blossom luck, which is associated with love and romance.

The Dog belongs to the alliance of Dog, Tiger and Horse, which has the Rabbit as their Peach Blossom link.

For the Dog, displaying Rabbit images in the home actualises romance and marriage luck.

The Dog benefits from placing the **Peach Blossom Rabbit** in the East part of the home or bedroom or in the Dog direction of NW.

5. Seasonal Trinities

Another grouping of signs creates the seasonal trinity combinations that bring the luck of *seasonal abundance*. To many experts, this is regarded as one of the more powerful combinations. When it exists within a family made up of either parent or both parents with one or more children, it indicates that as a family unit, their collective luck can transform all that is negative into positive outcomes. When annual indications of the year are not favourable, the existence of a seasonal combination of signs in any living abode can transform bad luck into better luck, especially during the season indicated by the combination.

It is necessary for all three signs to live together or be in the same office working in close proximity for this powerful pattern to work. For greater impact, it is

ANIMAL SIGNS	SEASON	ELEMEMT	DIRECTION
Dragon, Rabbit, Tiger	*Spring*	Wood	East
Snake, Horse, Sheep	*Summer*	Fire	South
Monkey, Rooster, Dog	*Autumn*	Metal	West
Ox, Rat, Boar	*Winter*	Water	North

Seasonal Trinities

better if they are all using the direction associated with the relevant season. The Dog belongs to the Autumn Season, its direction is West, and its seasonal group comprises the Monkey, Rooster and Dog.

6. Astrological Enemies

Your astrological enemy is the sign that directly confronts yours in the astrology wheel. For the Dog, your astrological enemy is the Dragon. Note that your enemy does not necessarily harm you; it only means someone of this sign can never be of any real help to you. There is a six-year gap between natural enemies. A marriage between astrological enemies is not usually recommended.

The Dog is advised to refrain from getting involved with anyone born in the year of the Dragon, although on a year-by-year basis, this can sometimes be

PAIRINGS OF ASTROLOGICAL ENEMIES		
Rat	⟷	Horse
Boar	⟷	Snake
Dog	⟷	Dragon
Rabbit	⟷	Rooster
Tiger	⟷	Monkey
Ox	⟷	Sheep

overcome by the annual energies. As a business partnership, this pairing is likely to lead to problems, and in the event of a split, the separation is often acrimonious.

Dog and Dragon are better off not marrying or living together as partners. Even when there is love between you in the early stages, you are unlikely to be close over the long term. Note however that astrological opposites can co-exist quite harmoniously as friends or siblings.

CURE: If a Dog is already married to a Dragon, the solution to improve your prospects for lasting happiness is to introduce the secret friend of each other into your living space. This can be done through the symbolic use of figurines or art. As a pair, you should display the secret friend of the Dragon, the **Rooster**, and the secret friend of the Dog, the **Rabbit**, in the home.

DOG with RAT

Success for these two in 2021

These two have no obvious natural affinity for one another, and no great loyalty either, but in 2021, this all changes. Dog and Rat's annual energies conspire for these two signs to come together, and should they do so, there is much success and satisfaction to be gained all round. While their relationship is better as friends or colleagues than lovers, there is no reason for this union not to work between the sheets, albeit likely for a short time.

Dog and Rat are both happy-go-lucky personalities filled with good humour, so they make excellent fair-weather friends. When the going is good, they are each other's champions, and they have a roaring good time with their mutual admiration turned on full blast. But unfortunately with these two, they are unlikely to stay when the going gets tough.

2021 causes a shift in their compatibility. For this year, their numbers form the Big Wealth Ho Tu, and thus especially when it comes to work, business and commerce, Dog and Rat working together yields fabulous results.

A wealthy pairing ★★★★

It works out better for Dog to take the lead this year, as the Rat is lacking in energy while Dog is filled with it. The Dog of 2021 will be more rottweiler than yorkshire terrier, while the Rat will prefer to revert to its nocturnal habits, enjoying the privacy and solitude of its own company and that of close friends and family.

> While Dog may feel more sociable than Rat, it benefits both to mix and mingle and to get out there, because there are great opportunities to be had by these two. What's more, when working together, they enjoy a very special brand of wealth luck, the kind that comes as a windfall.

For the Dog and Rat who are married, while there may be occasional personality clashes to deal with, they strive for a common goal. Whether their shared aspiration is a financial or domestic matter, their life goals align, which will help them overcome any conflict in approach in order to win their prize.

As siblings, Dog and Rat work better if not put in direct competition with one another. Parents of a pair of Dog and Rat should endeavour to nurture their individual interests, then they will end up supportive and nurturing of one another.

DOG with OX

A rocky road ahead for these two

Dog and Ox can make a good couple, but 2021 will not make this easy. Both are strong characters who often hold disparate views, so when the energies of the year are not with them, this will often blow up into arguments and conflict. The Ox can be dogmatic and stubborn, while the Dog can be aggressive and hostile, and unfortunately in 2021, the year brings out these traits when these two are together.

Dog and Ox's energies clash terribly this year, and too much time spent with one another only accentuates this fact.

If these two have only just met, it may be a good idea to take things slow. Not the best of times to go in too deep with one another. Dog and Ox will debate and argue all the time, and then one can really hurt the other. Don't let things become too ugly between you.

The Dog suffers from the betrayal and loss star, while the Ox has the influence of the magnification star. If Dog and Ox try to work together, neither will be good for the other. They could end up making a lot of bad mutual decisions, and each will try to blame the other when push comes to shove. Not a pleasant pairing at all in 2021.

As lovers, there is no lack of passion between a Dog and an Ox, but pleasure is tainted by pain. In this relationship, there will be plenty of ups and downs, so those wanting to enjoy the ups unfortunately have to also contend with plenty of downs, and some of them will be deep.

Dog and Ox make better friends than lovers, especially in this Year of the Ox. Both these signs are polite and well-mannered, so it will only become a problem if they get too close. Familiarity will breed contempt. But if they stay casual acquaintances, there is no reason why these two cannot work well together.

FENG SHUI CURE: For Dog and Ox to survive the year together, both need to carry the **Peace and Harmony Amulet** and work at being more tolerant.

Ox needs to overlook Dog's hostility, and Dog needs to control its temper. If Ox responds to Dog in an equally unfriendly way, things will spiral out of control. If this relationship is going to be bearable this year, it will be up to the Ox to be the bigger person.

DOG with TIGER

Taking on the world together

Dog and Tiger are astrological allies of the Zodiac and most definitely favourable for each other. They make an extremely cosy couple who not only enjoy each other's company but also bring out the best in each other. Between them flows great understanding and love. With each other, they are generous to a fault, and can end up loving each other more than themselves.

While 2021 will not be short of challenges for these two, together they face anything that arises with courage and perseverance.

They generate powerful synergy when together, transforming obstacles into opportunities. Whether they go through good times or bad, they come out better when they face them together.

As a couple, Dog and Tiger generate good hype and are socially popular. Being extroverts by nature, they are excellent at making friends and transforming business associates into life-long allies. Their great strength lies in their skills in networking. They easily make good contacts that can help them in their business and in generating goodwill. They thus make excellent business partners, able to build something successful and meaningful together. Both are motivated by high ideals and cherish the same values, so an inner bonding brings them closer with each passing year. In fact they can get fired up by injustices and relentlessly pursue causes they believe in. Their thought processes and attitude to life also make them easy to get along with.

Neither are overly sensitive or given to looking for people to blame when things go wrong. Both act out of impulse so there is none of the tension associated with formal presentations and hot shot planning sessions. They are happy to provide their own counsel and create their own inspiration.

The year ahead is a good time to strengthen their commitment to each other. Dog has to endure the negative afflictions associated with the *Robbery Star*, but Tiger's energy helps them as a couple.

In 2021, both enjoy a *Star of Small Auspicious*, which suggests that in all the small things, the tiny situations that make up the sum total of living, these two will enjoy a smooth year. This is the kind of energy conducive to people falling in love and staying in love.

DOG with RABBIT

So good for each other

Dog and Rabbit are always good for each other. They are secret friends of the Zodiac, so if they find one another in each other's lives, their relationship can quickly develop into great affection and deep love. The Rabbit in 2021 has all the energies of the Peach Blossom behind it, making it extremely attractive, and a Dog that crosses its path will hardly be able to resist.

The beautiful thing about a Dog and Rabbit pairing is their wonderful sympatico. They forgive each other's misgiving, almost blind to each other's faults, so when they are together, they bring out all that is good in one another.

The Dog in 2021 comes under the influence of the *Loss Star*, so it may not be going through the easiest of times, but with a Rabbit partner at its side, the Dog grows strong and resilient. The Rabbit falls in love easily this year, and with a Dog, it gains a partner who appreciates it for who it is. Their love for each other is thus incredibly and enduring.

When Dog and Rabbit succeed in getting married, theirs will be a satisfying life with the promise of great happiness. And even if they should separate or part for any reason, this is a couple who will usually stay good friends.

Dog and Rabbit can rely on each other in good times or bad, and the compatibility of their feelings and attitudes override all obstacles. Any attempt to split them or introduce suspicion between them is unlikely to work, and in 2021, Rabbit pulls Dog out of its troublesome periods.

As work mates or business partners, they bring out all that is creative in each other and there is a lot of mutual respect. The luck of the Rabbit trumps that of the Dog this year, so in this pair, Rabbit is likely to take the lead. Dog however is happy to follow without grumbles or complaint. Theirs is a partnership of equals, because even when one side agrees for the other to lead, its opinions are always carefully considered.

They make great friends and confidantes, and their conversations are always relaxed and easy-going. Should they come together as a couple, not only will their union be a happy one, they bring much success luck to one another as well.

DOG with DRAGON

Deep incompatibility worsens in 2021

Dog and Dragon are not good for one another. They bring out the worst in each other, constantly finding fault and causing all kinds of negative instincts to surface. They do not make a good couple either living or working together. Even if they do come together because of initial attraction, the superficiality of their relationship quickly becomes evident. It will be difficult for a Dog and Dragon relationship to last beyond a few first dates.

The only way this union will work well is if at least one has the ascendant of the other in its birth chart. If one of them is born in the hour of the other e.g. if the Dog is born in the hour of the Dragon (7am to 9am), or Dragon is born in the hour of the Dog (7pm to 9pm).

The other way to fix a bad union that has already happened is to form the Earth Cross within the family. If a pair of Dog and Dragon parents have children born in the Ox and Sheep here, the four signs together create good fortune. But this does not mean Dragon and Dog will get along; it simply means their joint success together smooths things over in their personal relationship.

True compatibility between a Dog and Dragon is difficult to achieve, and this is even more so in 2021, when neither are going through an easy year.

In 2021, Dragon suffers from the Five Yellow affliction, so will have its fair share or troubles to deal with. Dog meanwhile has the Loss Star in its sector. Both will be too busy fixing their own problems to give much time or comfort to the other.

With the Dog, Dragon's courage and valour becomes foolhardiness; with the Dragon, Dog's loyalty becomes neediness. Neither brings out what is positive in the other, and instead, transforms strengths into negatives. Not a good match.

Dog is disdainful of Dragon's ideas and opinions; and Dragon finds Dog unsupportive and a wet blanket. This match is a classic example of clashing personalities. Not only is there little communication, there is much exhaling in exasperation on the part of the Dragon, and a great deal of barking from the Dog! Better look elsewhere for a better match if you are looking for long-term happiness.

DOG with SNAKE

Little chemistry between these two

Dog and Snake are two signs that are extremely pleasant to, and about, each other. Between them there is plenty of mutual respect, but they work better as colleagues or business partners than as lovers or spouses, simply because it is difficult to ignite a great passion between them. There is some compatibility, just not of the romantic kind.

If they come together as a married couple, their life will be reasonably stable and happy, but there is an ordinariness which makes them vulnerable to externally stimulated promises of excitement. When the slightest opportunity arises or when the energy of the year encourages it, either party could be unfaithful. Snake and Dog couples who are going through some kind of mid-life crisis could well find themselves being distracted or tempted to look for love outside their marriage.

This relationship generally works out better for the Snake than the Dog. If infidelity arises, it will more likely come from the Snake, because Dogs tend to be infinitely more faithful. The Dog may well forgive the Snake should it stray. Indeed they are so good at adapting to whatever situation presents itself that no matter what Snake does or does not do, Dog will always come round to Snake's way of thinking. From this point of view, a pairing with the Dog is not necessary a bad match for the Snake. It depends on what the Snake is looking for, but if it is excitement, it is unlikely to find it in the arms of a Dog. For the Dog, being married to a Snake may make it constantly feel insecure.

In 2021, the year brings mixed indications for this pairing. Both have troublesome flying stars to deal with, but also auspicious indications from the 24 Mountains.

If they focus on achieving success together, they can make a good team. But there is little indication of much romance or passion, and Snake may get restless as the year unfolds.

FENG SHUI CURE: A Dog and Snake pairing benefits from carrying the **Enhancing Relationships Amulet** and displaying **Marriage Happiness Ducks** in the home. If they have been "drifting apart", it is a good idea to put more effort into the relationship, or infidelity could become an unpleasant reality.

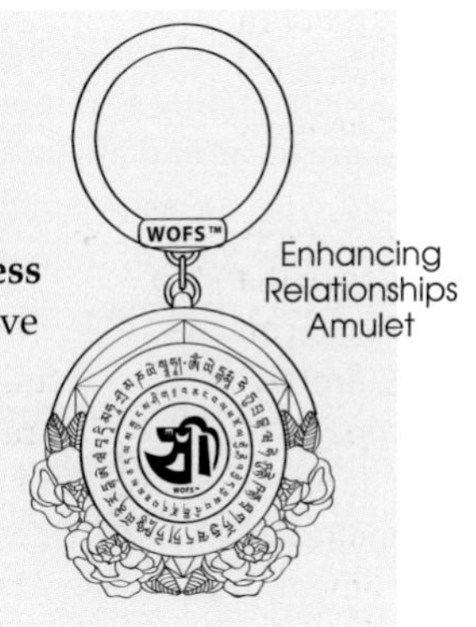

Enhancing Relationships Amulet

DOG with HORSE

Two individuals motivated by the same things

Dog and Horse are astrological allies of the Zodiac, so these two are good for each other no matter the year or circumstance. A Dog and Horse who get married will build a fabulous family life together. Both will put family first, no matter how busy or successful they become outside the home. Both are family-oriented individuals who have plenty of time for the family.

In 2021, Dog has the loss star in its chart, but with a Horse partner, there is nothing Dog cannot weather. Horse imbues Dog with lots of courage and perseverance.

Between Dog and Horse, there always flows a lot of understanding and love. These two signs find it easy to share ideas and assets, and go through good times and bad with the same spirit of give and take. They share the same kind of humour and are able to walk through difficult challenges.

They generate powerful synergy to take advantage of whatever opportunities may open up for them. In a year when Horse enjoys not one but two *Big Auspicious* stars, with Dog enjoying a *Small Auspicious*, they make a dynamic and promising duo indeed.

They are socially popular and will find that they like the same types of people. Dog and Horse generate good hype as a couple and as a result, their social life is excellent. Both being extroverts by nature, they are good at making friends and transforming business associates into life-long allies. Their great strength is in networking, making good contacts that help them in business and in generating goodwill. In commercial pursuits, they collaborate very well.

These are two people motivated by high ideals. They cherish the same values so there is an inner bonding that brings them closer with each passing year. They get fired up and relentlessly pursue causes they believe in. They think alike with neither being overly sensitive or given to looking to blame the other should things go wrong.

They act out of impulse so there is usually no heavy discussion of serious issues between them. Their interactions are rarely if ever tense, and they are happy to do away with formality. These are instant decision makers and rightly or wrongly, they are happy to bumble their way through life, to be their own counsel and to create their own inspiration.

DOG with SHEEP

A happy pairing in 2021

These two Earth signs enjoy moderate affinity with one another. While not entirely compatible, with differing personalities and life goals, they can make a relationship between them work because they are able to agree to disagree. Neither is particularly insistent on taking charge, so they will share the honours. While there's unlikely to be any grand passion, they can make a very cordial and accommodating pair.

In 2021, these two Earth signs are helped by their luck stars, which combine to bring them much shared good fortune.

In work and business, Dog and Sheep make great strides together in 2021. They are more productive and find each other a good sounding board whenever they need to formulate strategy and new ideas. Sheep's creativity gets a great boost with the loyal Dog's constant applause.

The nice thing about this relationship is the lack of jealousy or malice. They never feel like that towards each other. Even when pitted against each other for any reason, they can wear two hats - that of competitors and that of supporters. Neither is a sore loser, nor does one insist on taking the credit or hogging the limelight.

In a love relationship, things are easier if the stakes in any difference of opinion are not too high. It also helps if Sheep allows Dog to make the difficult decisions, and is able to fall in with plans submissively.

In socialising with outside parties, both are excellent in keeping friends and making others feel comfortable with them, so as a couple they will be popular, with an extensive network of contacts and allies. Life together is usually very pleasant.

This pair should enjoy a relatively harmonious year with no major disruptions. There is good affinity in their chi energies and for once, they are communicating on the same wavelength as there is much common ground. Indeed there is more that link them than pull them apart.

While this may not be a usual pairing, things are helped very much in 2021 by the annual energies. If Dog and Sheep fall in love this year, romance will play a big part. You don't get any sign as romantic as the dreamy Sheep. The nice thing in this union is that the Dog will appreciate all of Sheep's thoughtfulness and advances. There is plenty of mutual attraction here.

DOG with MONKEY

A good year but danger of infidelity

Dog and Monkey are not the most passionate of couples. They can be friends and even married to one another, and their relationship can last, but this union lacks the fire that fuels other pairings. In a marriage, these two generally lead their own lives, growing apart yet staying together. But there are no noisy fights as both have good control over their tempers. They react with cold silence rather than go into a shouting match. This can be a sustainable match, but borne out of convenience rather than deep love.

In 2021, the luck profiles of Dog and Monkey sync up well, so these two signs can achieve much success together. Their sum-of-ten luck suggest that should they team up in a work capacity this year, they can achieve a lot.

Monkey's element luck is far stronger than Dog's this year, so Monkey will be the one in the driver's seat. But Dog is appreciative and loyal to whatever plan Monkey has up its sleeve. As colleagues or partners, they make a very good team. While their personalities differ, they fit very well together where one naturally assumes the leadership role, and the other deputies very well. Here you will not get frequent clashes of will, because even when they disagree, they resolve things very quickly, as the Dog will always back down.

Monkey is feeling strong this year and exudes an extremely charismatic air, something that is sure to pull Dog in. It will be difficult for a Dog to resist a Monkey who means to win him or her over. But this is a good match this year. Between Dog and Monkey, they can expect to see a whole series of small but very tangible successes. Building for the future also becomes easy, as they find their longer term goals aligning.

The danger for a Dog and Monkey pairing this year will be the External Star of Romance. This brings the hazard of infidelities in marriages, and between these two, because passion is lukewarm at best, temptation may lure one or the other to stray.

CURE: For the Dog-Monkey couple who are married, it is wise to place marriage enhancers in the home and to wear the **Marriage Saver Amulet** to prevent outsiders from causing problems in the marriage. And place a pair of **Marriage Happiness Ducks** in the SW.

DOG with ROOSTER

Moderate affinity between these two

Dog and Rooster are poles apart in terms of personality yet they can form the firmest of friendships. In fact, once they are pals, the loyal Dog will stand beside its Rooster mate no matter what the cost, and no matter who's in the right or wrong. While Dog is somewhat righteous believing in strict moral codes, with a Rooster, a Dog is willing to break even the law.

Dog and Rooster make better friends than lovers. Any love relationship they have will tend to be characterised more by warmth and loyalty than by passion.

There is little excitement when it comes to a Dog and Rooster love affair, but they can build a stable and secure married life. That is, till one succumbs to temptation. Infidelities, if any, will likely come from the Rooster, although under certain circumstances, the Dog can also stray. The lack of passion between them makes them vulnerable to advances from third parties, so when temptation knocks, they could well make a mistake. In 2021, the *Star of External Romance* poses this kind of threat. Happily, these two can forgive careless dalliances if they are convinced they are nothing more than a lusty blunder.

Dog and Rooster make a better pairing in business. Dog will often be in awe of Rooster's capabilities, and will thus endure the pontifications of the Rooster. Rooster can then be as productive and as ingenious as it wants without being stalled by a insecure partner. Dog genuinely identifies positively with Rooster's high ideals and quest for perfection, so will be both understanding and tolerant. There are more than enough ingredients therefore for a happy and productive team between these two.

As friends, these two share the kind of relationship where they can spend years apart then come back together like nothing at all has changed. They are also seasonal friends of the Zodiac, sharing the season of Autumn together. This indicates that with each other, they have windows of opportunity to achieve great success and to earn great wealth.

In 2021, Rooster has the wealth star and Dog has *Small Auspicious* from the 24 Mountains. Their luck patterns and their affinity point to a successful year together should they team-up.

DOG with DOG

Celebrating small success together

Dog-born are usually sensitive to their spouses and also considerate as individuals, so when two Dogs get together, it does not seem likely that they will have any major differences of opinion. In fact, when a Dog marries another Dog, they tend to bring out the more congenial aspects of the other's personality. They live just as happily when they live fairly self-sufficiently, with each partner doing their own thing and carving out independent careers.

Two Dogs are neither competitive nor judgemental with each other, each respecting the personal space, aspirations and eccentricities of the other.

When two Dogs make a home together, they soon find their respective comfort levels and even their own corners within the home, so there should be continuing harmony in their domestic household.

Dogs usually prefer the well-trodden path. Neither side has the adventurous streak that urges them to take off for the other side of the world at a moment's notice, but should someone suggest it, they will not be averse to doing so. Inside a marriage however, both prefer the quiet and stable life rather than trekking the big wide world. They will put in every effort to build a comfortable home where neither particularly want to ever leave. This is the foundation of this pair, so although most signs do not get along well with their own signs, a Dog is quite happy living with another Dog.

In 2021, Dog goes through a moderate year with some success indications, including a *Small Auspicious* star from the 24 Mountains. This brings happy occasions into their house. They can stay at home and enjoy the comforts it provides and be perfectly content. The small luck star can also denote wealth, prosperity, the arrival of a child or the marriage of someone dear.

While this may not be a year when the big breaks come for the Dog couple, there will be many small successes along the way which create stepping stones for a brighter future.

Two Dogs know how to enjoy life, so they will see the most positive side of everything, and in 2021, every success is given adequate attention and applause. Two Dogs together are very supportive of one another, and can be each other's lead cheerleader.

DOG with BOAR

Soulmates weathering a difficult year

These two share the *Zodiac House of Domesticity* together, which spells good things for this pair. Belonging to the same house gives two signs exceptional affinity, so whatever they get up to will bring both a great deal of happiness. But 2021 brings some problems.

In 2021, Dog and Boar both get afflicted by the Betrayal Star #7, which causes all kinds of arguments to take place and even for dishonesty to creep into the picture.

In view of this, Boar or Dog, or both, could lose interest in the relationship. Having the *Betrayal Star* brings hard times, so if there are problems between them, they must remember that underlying all the negativity, there is genuine caring for each other.

Boar knows that very few things cause Dog to lose sight of what makes existence meaningful. But Dog does have a tendency to preach, occasionally getting on its high horse to lecture those close to it about anything and everything. Boar cannot take this and eventually starts to see the Dog as a tiresome nag! When things get too tiresome, Boar could very well trot off into the sunset.

This is not a bad relationship as these two signs enjoy a genuine mutual love, but Dog and Boar are not insanely passionate about each other. There is instead a lovely warmth between them - and thus it is important that this coziness does not get shattered by too much nagging and lecturing.

In the event of a rift, note that Dog and Boar are two of the Zodiac's signs who dislike noisy quarrels, so in this year of trials and tribulations, it is possible that both could simply throw their hands up in the air and leave it to the passage of time to clear the energies.

Dog benefits from Boar's philosophy of *cest la vie,* adopting a carefree attitude towards life in general and opting to cope with whatever comes in a relaxed manner. But there is sincerity in this pairing and both are genuinely agreeable. Boar does not judge Dog in any way, and it is good for the Dog to reciprocate in like manner.

In no time at all, the year with all its discordant chi casting a negative pall on these two will be over. But while living through it, Dog will take great comfort in having someone like the Boar to lean on. It is just important for both sides to appreciate the special affinity both have, and not allow anything to spoil their great potential.

Dog's Monthly Horoscope 2021

Chapter 6

Helping others awakens something special in the Dog

The Dog faces a mixed year when your luck is neither very good nor very bad. Your luck elements indicate you won't be short of opportunities, but to attain success, you will need patience and staying power. Results won't come overnight, so those who want success have to persevere and grow a thick skin. There will be detractors who discourage you or pour cold water over your ideas; try not to spend too much time in the company of such people. The productive Dog is the one that is happy, and the Dog is happiest when doing good, so look for a noble cause to direct your energies towards. Helping those less fortunate than you is what will awaken the passion you need to succeed in all other spheres of your life in 2021.

1st Month
February 4th - March 5th 2021

UNSEEN HAND HELPING YOU. LISTEN TO YOUR HEART.

While this is not a year in which the Dog can expect too much, there is nevertheless good progress to be made. Your final goals may take longer to achieve, but you can make good headway if you adopt the right attitude. Look at the glass half full, spot the positive in everything, keep friends that make you feel valued, distance yourself from those who don't. If you adopt some simple rules to living, the year will march on at a happy pace. What the Dog needs is to feel motivated. If your job does not stimulate you, think seriously about making a change. Or find something else in your life to add energy and sparkle to your being. For most Dogs, social work is a natural calling. Get involved in something that lets you change the world for the better!

Work & Career - *Thinking about the future*

There is good news on the horizon either in the form of a promotion or upgrade in your work situation. Someone more senior may notice you and take you under their wing. If not entirely satisfied with your job, you may be spotted by an outside company and head-hunted. Or go looking yourself. Think carefully before making such decisions, as you may not be able to go back. Be realistic about a career change. But you can afford to listen to your instincts. If your heart says do it, take courage from this. But if you have that gnawing feeling you'd be throwing something good away, think twice.

You can listen to your heart, but don't burn any bridges. Value every connection you have made over the years.

Business - *Allies, mentors and good ideas*
A good month for those running your own business or helming a large company. You have allies in the right places willing to bend backwards to accommodate your wishes! Make full use of resources and rake in the lush rewards! Brainstorming with colleagues throws out some great ideas, so do this often. New ventures suggest themselves, and why not pursue them! If the stakes are not high and you feel good about something, go for it!

A good time to nurture a sapling idea, but remember - saplings take time to grow, so don't be impatient! The more social you are, the better. You never know who you will meet or what opportunities they will bring. Sometimes the biggest breaks come in unexpected guises and from surprising sources. Use your naturally friendly persona to enlarge your friendship circles.

Love & Relationships - *Good energy*

You are a fun bundle of energy, so you are in for a rollicking great time. Single Dogs are in high demand with plenty of admirers, more so when you turn on the charm. Enjoy your popularity and sex appeal but don't let it get to your head. Keep your feet firmly on the ground lest you get swept away by the temporary euphoria. People flatter you, but accept such compliments graciously and at surface value. While affairs of the heart turn you on now, they are far from being your only concern. On a positive level, you find you are attracted to brains more than beauty. Whoever attracts your attention now must also pass your soulmate test, as whether you acknowledge it or not, you're looking for someone you could "end up with".

Home & Family - *Building a family*

Auspicious time to start a new family or plan for a new child as babies conceived this period will bring joy and honour to the family. For young Dogs, pay particular attention to advice from your parents this month.

School & Education - *Motivated*

It's easy for the young Dog to muster up plenty of enthusiasm for their studies now, so parents of Dog children in school have it easy. The Dog student is feeling particularly motivated. When you unlock this feeling, recognize what's causing it, then engineer so you have more of whatever is making you feel good.

2nd Month
March 6th - April 4th 2021

DIFFICULT & CHALLENGING TIMES AHEAD

The *Five Yellow* arrives to disturb the peace and put a spanner in the works. Coupled with the *Loss Star*, things could get stressful, especially for those heavily invested in the stock market, with open positions, or with something big to lose. Rivals edge ahead of you at work and in other competitive situations, and it may seem that the harder you try, the more difficult it becomes to salvage something for yourself. Don't attract too much attention or you'll make yourself a target. In conversation, you find your counterparts more disagreeable than usual and what's frustrating is that onlookers don't seem to see your point of view. Quit trying to win this month. Luck is not on your side. Best you can do is work to mitigate the damage.

Work & Career - *Stay low profile*

The office seems saturated with ill-talk and malicious gossip. You feel stressed out from overwork and becoming a target of office gossip. Even so, try to keep quiet and not retaliate as certain things you say in the heat of the moment may be used against you later.

Keep private information to yourself. Don't confide in anyone unless you want it to be broadcast. Work feels exhausting and if things get any worse, you may wish to reconsider what else you can do. A short break away to clear the mind would do you a world of good, and your absence could deflect the arrows of antagonism aimed your way.

Stay above the fray. Keep a low profile and don't attract too much attention. The lower your profile, the better you will feel.

Business - *Take a step back*
Business slackens and it seems difficult to meet objectives. Managing the workforce feels like you are pulling teeth. If you're heading the charge, it feels as if you need more patience than you have, as nobody seems to be on the same page as you. Instead of coming against arguments in every meeting, take a step back. Allow your generals to take the reins and lay the responsibility on them. When your luck is down, that could be your best move, whoever the major stakeholders ultimately are. Keep your options open. Avoid venturing into new territory and stay away from risk-taking. Avoid signing big contracts or putting money into risky schemes, as they may not work out. This is a time to consolidate rather than expand. Look inwards for new opportunities rather than outwards.

Be careful of getting played out. You can get cheated by people who seem above board as your wealth luck is diluted.

Love & Relationships - *Unstable*

Irritations can be expected in your love life. Those in relationships could find themselves on unstable ground. Misunderstandings aggravate an already fragile sentiment. You feel like you're being taken for a ride, so a heart-to-heart talk may be needed to clear the air. If you're single and seeking a soulmate, best to wait till the month is over. Not a good time to go steady, as even if someone seems right for you now, that may no longer be the case as the month unfolds. Avoid getting married this month. With love luck so strained, you should give affairs of the heart a break and put your energies elsewhere.

Education - *Don't get distracted*

School life is not a bed of roses as you suffer low energy levels. Plan your time efficiently. You seem to have only temporary bursts of energy, so you must make use of such brief periods to do as much as possible .

CURE FOR THE MONTH: All Dogs should carry the **Five Element Pagoda Amulet** this month. Those venturing out at night need the **Nightspot Protection Amulet**.

3rd Month
April 5th - May 5th 2021

FEELING CREATIVE. MANY GOOD IDEAS UP YOUR SLEEVE.

Much better month than last! Your ideas are finally going somewhere. People listen when you share them and the nice thing is that they work out, so they help your credibility. The energies particularly suit students and those involved in learning and research. Your powers of communication increase, and people sit up and listen when you speak. A good time for those in leadership positions or vying for a spot in the limelight. Also a fabulous month for love and all things romantic! The more relaxed you are, the better things work out for you. Don't let small complications get you down. Why worry when you can change things, and why worry when you can't? Taking this philosophy to heart will ensure you come out of the month ahead of where you start it.

Work & Career - *Making great strides*

You're extremely likeable now because you have the knack of saying just the right thing. Sometimes even when you have the best of intentions, things come out wrong, but not this month! You make all the right moves, and everyone is flocking to be your friend. At work, you're as popular with your peers as with the boss, so even as you get ahead, there are no jealousies to rain on your parade. A month when you make good progress career-wise. The right eyes are on you so you want to make a good impression. The best way to do that is to stay professional, but also stay relaxed.

Your energy levels are recharged and you are ready for anything. You can achieve a lot now if you put your mind to work properly.

Business - *Stay well-informed*

Keep abreast of all that is happening around you. Make well-informed decisions based on sound research. Trust your instincts but also what the facts and figures are telling you. Take the most logical approach and you won't go far wrong. Lead your team by example. Be hands on and mingle with the mainstream staff instead of just the elite few of you. Brainstorming sessions with entire team can throw out marvellous ideas and help shore up morale. Some business competitors may resort to underhand tactics; you can either respond with a taste of their own medicine or let the quality of your goods and services speak for themselves. Work on building relationships, as this is an area where you excel with the help of the #4 relationship star.

Love & Relationships - *Passionate*

Passion overflows and you can flirt to your heart's content. Everything goes well when it comes to love, and even better when you take the lead. Singles will have every chance to settle down, but you may be having such a good time playing the field you may not want to! Go for it if you've found the right person, but don't let yourself get rushed into anything. If not sure, save your declarations of eternal love for another time. The only danger this month comes in the form of infidelity on your part. Dogs are not natural philanderers, but this month temptation may come your way. Be careful you don't throw away something good for a short window of fun.

Education - *Aim high*

The student Dog can set high personal standards as you are well poised to meet them. A great opportunity exists for you to leapfrog to the next level, so go for it! Aim for the very top, not just the top half of the class.

ENHANCER FOR THE MONTH: Carry the **Windhorse Success Amulet** this month. All kinds of opportunities await you and having the Windhorse near will ensure you can take advantage of them.

4th Month
May 6th - June 5th 2021

LESS AGREEABLE BUT YOU GET THE JOB DONE. BE KIND.

A lucky month, only marred by the *Quarrelsome Star* in your chart. You enjoy the *Sum-of-Ten* which brings you completion luck. Things you start can get finished in magnificent fashion. In your quest for success, watch you don't step on too many toes. They will not make a fuss now, but you can earn yourself some sleeper enemies who rear their ugly heads when you're most vulnerable. Control your temper and be generous when you do well. Share your successes and give credit where it is due. You have more than enough accolades being piled on you, it's nice to share some of the glory; else you could fall victim to the "Tall Poppy" syndrome.

Work & Career - *Don't make enemies*

There is tension in the office but nothing you cannot handle. You may be stressed out about an excessive workload, but now is the time to prove you can handle anything thrown at you. You're productive although you may not be the most pleasant to work with. In your prickly mood, watch you don't make enemies. Getting on the wrong side of the wrong person could cause them to undermine you any chance they get. Keep the **Apple Peace Amulet** near you or better still, place the **Rooster with Crown** on your work desk to control the #3 star hovering over you.

Business - *Not people-friendly*

Your dealings with people in positions of power are lackluster, so avoid applying for licences, tenders, contracts or anything connected with governmental bureaucracy. Not a people-friendly month, so rein in your temper and be more tolerant of others. Focus on projects you have on hand and work on finishing them rather than scouting for new ones. Your mood is not conducive to negotiation and you are likely to upset others with too much interaction. Your frame of mind means you should avoid high level meetings as you may offend important people who find it hard to forgive. Prepare the foundations for future expansion, but hold off taking on anything too new for now.

Love & Relationships - *Don't make jokes*

Love is not half as fun as it was last month, so this could come as a rude awakening. It may feel like your libido suddenly got switched off, but a lot of this could be due to your overly sharp tongue which has the knack of spoiling the mood. Watch what you say. Don't offend for the sake of doing so. And remember, jokes made at someone else's expense is rarely funny for all sides. Don't make jokes about your partner, or worse, someone you are trying to date. When the deal is not yet sealed, behaving badly is the surest way to prematurely end a relationship. If what you have with someone is important to you, be careful what you say around them. Those single who haven't yet met anyone, may need to wait a little longer. This month is not conducive to fairy-tale romances.

Home & Family - *Correct the NW*

If family harmony is being affected by your funny mood this month, check the NW of the home. Don't have too much noise or action in this sector and place a **Red Carpet with Auspicious Symbols** here to press down on the difficult energies occupying your home sector.

Education - *Feeling competitive*

Friends may grate your nerves when you are rushing to complete assignments, and you are feeling especially competitive. Your intense focus may cause you to temporarily fall out with friends; don't worry yourself too much. If grades are more important to you than to your pals, there will be a mismatch of aspirations. Take a break from your social circle till your work is done. Don't let peer pressure sway you from what matters most to you.

CURE FOR THE MONTH: Carry the **Apple Peace Amulet**. For those facing politics at the workplace, carry the **Kuan Kung on Horseback Anti-Betrayal Amulet** and display a **Rooster with Crown** on your workdesk.

5th Month
June 6th - July 6th 2021

"BIG WEALTH" HO TU BUT LACKING STRENGTH TO FOLLOW THROUGH

Ups and downs characterise this month. Life is extremely promising when it comes to commercial ventures and making money, but your health suffers. You are exposed to the illness star, so elderly Dog people especially need to be more careful. The 39-year-old Water Dog also needs to beware, as element health luck is very poor for you this year. Lucrative opportunities may be tempting but don't let work triumph at the expense of your health. Things can get serious quickly if you ignore warning signs. Go for regular check-ups if you fall under a high-risk category. If contagious diseases (e.g. COVID-19) are still plaguing the world, take the necessary precautions. Don't be too casual when it comes to your health.

Work & Career - *Finding shortcuts*

You are loaded with work which you can normally handle, but now you begin to feel under the weather. Falling sick when you have work worries is a bad combination! Delegate wherever possible. Get others involved and don't try to get everything done by yourself. Recruit other colleagues to help. If you're a team player, others will be willing to chip in. Work smart rather than hard since your health is not up to par. If you bother to look for short cuts, you will find quite a few. Outsmarting the slow slog could also reduce the number of careless mistakes you make from working too hard too long.

You are more prone to falling sick this month, so pay some attention to your health.

Business - *Promising*

You enjoy the *Big Wealth Ho Tu* this month. This is good news as it means you have the potential to do extremely well commercially. For some, this indication points to some kind of breakthrough. Activate with the **Ho Tu Enhancer** placed in the NW or anywhere on your work desk. With this kind of luck, you can be more courageous when taking risks. But plan properly. Make use of your whole team. Boost productivity in all your departments. And then set up scaling up your business. Don't try to do everything yourself. That way you save yourself from burnout, but also tap into the ideas of those more energetic than you; this could also help you uncover your next superstar who will allow you to halve your workload while doubling your output.

Love & Relationships - *Tender & romantic*

Hardly sizzling but not stone cold either. In fact, quite tender and heartwarming. You're more into quiet nights in with your sweetheart than wild nights on the town. Your energy levels point to romantic dinners with fine wine rather than tequila on the dance floor. Singles have many hopefuls sniffing around you. Don't analyze too much. Go with the flow. If something is meant to happen, let it. There are no rules you need to abide by. Follow your heart. You will know when someone is right for you, and when you do, don't be overly cautious. There is much happiness in store.

Health & Wellness - *Live healthy*

Develop a healthy routine. Try to fit in regular exercise no matter how busy you get. Carving out some time each day to keep yourself in good shape will end up increasing your productivity and output.

Education - *Relax*

School may seem more tedious, only because you are not feeling your best. Take heart that no one can produce constant flawless performance, and neither is it expected. Learn to relax and you will do even better.

CURE FOR THE MONTH: Since your major affliction this month is illness, you should invoke the **Medicine Buddha** by carrying his amulet, or carry the **Health Talisman Holder**.

6th Month
July 7th - Aug 7th 2021

CHANGES CHARACTERISE THE MONTH. CAN START NEW PROJECTS.

The *Victory Star* ushers in tidings of change for the Dog. This is a time of exciting new beginnings. If you've been weary from too much work or too hectic a schedule, now is when you get the opportunity to recharge. Book a short holiday away somewhere - it will do you a world of good! You're feeling a lot stronger and more enthusiastic this month and can really follow up on the opportunities that presented themselves last month. You're energetic and in a great mood, and this rubs off on everyone around you. You attract more of what you are, so keep up your good spirits. Follow your passions and don't let convention hold you back.

Work & Career - *Pioneer*

Things go your way and the path to success seems paved with gold. You get the chance to do something new that has never been done before, so you appear a pioneer. A time when you get to leave your mark! Accept all opportunities offered to you. Even if you feel unsure you're up to the task, you learn fast, and nothing is too much for you now. There are many willing to help if you only look. Some of you may be headhunted or offered an alternative, and if you're thinking of a career switch, you can seriously consider it. Your luck holds up well. But before you take the plunge, be sure, as there is no turning back.

Be prepared to take some risks, as nothing ventured, nothing gained. You have victory luck on your side, so success is very attainable.

Business - *Windows of opportunity*
Good time to make money as business opportunities that have been eluding you now appear on the horizon. Seize them as they appear. Some windows of opportunity may be fleeting, so don't rest on your laurels. Swap ideas with your people, get their opinions and ask if they have better ways to implement things. Check out new technology; you may find some that make life far more efficient or which can revolutionize your business. This is a fast-changing world and you have to be prepared to adapt. No better time to make drastic changes than now. You are blessed with a natural mantle to lead this month, so spend some time on this aspect of yourself. Get to know your staff, even those who don't work directly for you. A little motivation from you counts for a lot.

Love & Relationships - *Blooming*

A month filled with exciting promises of great things to come! Love blooms and romances take off. Those single have the best options as you have no one to answer to. Take the lead when it comes to connecting with those who catch your fancy. Whether man or woman, you can make the first move! Don't let the good ones get away. A good time to actively pursue a new relationship, or even rekindle an old one. You can really turn on the charm when you want, and when you do, others find you irresistible! You have such powers of attraction you can have almost anyone you desire, so go for it. As long as you make the effort, they should reciprocate.

Education - *Forging ahead*

Anything new you sink your teeth in will take off. Whether working on assignments, projects or trying to perfect a new skill, you make excellent progress and are likely to get noticed as a standout star. You are receptive to new ideas, so tune in and learn something new. Add to your extracurricular repertoire, or read more widely on subjects that already interest you.

ENHANCER FOR THE MONTH: Enhance the Victory Star with the **Victory Banner Success Amulet**. This will ensure you stay ahead, especially for those involved in competitive industries or in situations where coming out top is important to you.

7th Month
Aug 8th - Sept 7th 2021

BETRAYALS POSSIBLE.

The magnification star plays havoc with the energies in your chart, increasing the likelihood of getting betrayed or let down by friends and those close to you. Nothing will be done to seriously harm you, but it will hurt. Give the benefit of the doubt when you can, although the world through your rose-tinted glasses may no longer look so rosy. Don't hold on to grudges once you have forgiven, as they affect you more than the other party. At work, watch your back. Rivals pop up even among previous allies. Things change quickly so it is best to stay alert and to adapt yourself accordingly. There is no need to share everything with everyone. The Dog personality is honest to a fault, but this month it may be a good idea to hold some things back.

Work & Career - *Leaving your comfort zone*

There may be significant developments at work that thrust you out of your comfort zone. This could cause events to unfold one of two ways; you could find yourself out of your depth, or you could find your forte and impress all the right people. How successful you are depends on how committed you are. Seize opportunities that come your way rather than let them pass you by. If you need to seek advice with regards to work, be sure to go to someone you trust. There are hidden agendas you may be unaware of. This month it may be better to rely on your own instincts, as you are in danger of getting played out by others.

Watch your back and beware hidden enemies. You could get backstabbed by a friend, or someone you thought you could trust.

Business - *Be careful*

Good business opportunities come your way, but be careful when dealing with individuals you do not know well. Do not be too trusting and do ample research before entering into any new venture. If you are smart, you can secure yourself some good deals. Do not take your decisions lightly. Get involved in the daily operations of your work and make it a point to familiarise yourself even with the minute details of your business. When it comes to investing, better hold off for now. You have little luck when it comes to anything that involves taking a gamble. Playing it safe and conservative is your best strategy.

Love & Relationships - *Beware*

While you find yourself showered with plenty of attention, don't let it cloud your judgment. There is danger of getting betrayed by a friend. Beware excessive drinking or partying, which could make you vulnerable. Not everyone has savoury intentions, and in the heat of the moment, you could ignore even your own better judgement. If someone was unsuitable before, they probably still are. Those in relationships need to beware the threat of "external" romance. Infidelity is a real danger, and could afflict either you, or your partner, or both.

Home & Safety - *Check security*

As the *Robbery Star* gets enhanced, best to double check the security of your home. Make sure you shut windows and doors at night, check your CCTV is working, and avoid throwing house parties.

Education - *Tackle tasks one at a time*

A lot to get done at school but don't sweat; all can be accomplished if you tackle your tasks one by one. The hard part will be getting started. Remember that done is better than perfect when perfect is not done!

CURE FOR THE MONTH: Place the **28 Hums Protection Wheel with Heart Sutra** in the NW this month. You can also carry the portable version for protection at all times.

8th Month
Sept 8th - Oct 7th 2021

WEALTH LUCK INDICATED. COMMERCIAL VENTURES PROMISING.

The Prosperity Star arrives bringing plenty of wealth luck. Making money becomes less of an uphill climb. New opportunities open up and you start enjoying the fruits of your labour. You can take some risks and for sure can indulge in some lavish personal pampering! This is an auspicious month when living it up will not harm you, but will actually attract in even more good chi. When you have some spare cash, don't be averse to spending it. Give yourself a treat every now and then. This kind of prosperity programming is especially useful when your luck is headed upwards!

Work & Career - *Going great guns*

Things improve at work as all your plans seem ripe for success. You find your role at the office expanding, and the more you take on, the better you get at your job. A time when everything you touch turns to gold! Those in jobs where remuneration is commission-based may see a big jump in income. You have support from all the right quarters and important people who may not have taken notice of you in the past start to recognise your talents. Some may try and manipulate you to ride on your good luck, so be wary of anyone who appears a smidgen too friendly. All those broad smiles and pats on your back may be a prelude to a little back-stabbing! Concentrate on work rather than appearances; listen to the grapevine as you may learn something juicy but be a listener rather than a contributor.

Good fortune luck is immense. Your career is likely to see some form of major improvement.

Business - *Thank the right people*

Business luck is good, allowing you to plan with confidence and with much better peace of mind. While things may not yet be what they were in the past, they are getting there. A good time to make strategic changes in direction and to invest for the future. Remember to keep your plans medium to long term, because the big results will not come instantly. A month when you can win contracts and close deals heavily in your favour. Don't forget to celebrate your successes and thank all the right people. When you give praise where praise is due, you win over allies for life. The more such allies you have, the more effective and productive you can be. While wealth luck is riding high, if you wish to make even more money, do consider some donations to worthwhile charities. Giving away money when it comes easily makes room for you to make even more.

Love & Relationships - *Get things going!*

Love is in the air for the Dog, who is a big romantic at heart. Those in steady relationships, or embarking on a new one can take it to the next level. Don't be averse to declaring your love. If your relationship seems to be stuck on some kind of plateau, it is up to you to get things going again. Take the lead because your partner is just waiting for you to show the way. Because love luck is good, this is the best time for Dogs to find true love. If you haven't yet met the person of your dreams, and you want to, start actively looking!

Education - *Tap brains*

Tap the brains of teachers and friends. You have a lot going for you and any extra assistance will help you get those top grades you desire.

ENHANCER FOR THE MONTH: Keep the **Asset Wealth Bull** near you so the money you make this month can last into the future.

9th Month
Oct 8th - Nov 6th 2021

DOUBLE LOSS INDICATED. DO NOT TAKE RISKS.

Everything doubles up this month, with the month stars aligning up with the annual stars. Unfortunately for the Dog, this means a period of double loss. A month when you can lose money easily, so avoid investment of any kind. Definitely do not speculate or gamble since there is no luck here. Best to stay low key and not do too much. Always put safety first and think several steps ahead. Your luck is down so you must use your wits to get by. Depend on yourself and don't expect too much help from others. And definitely do not expect goodies to fall into your lap.

Work & Career - *Office politics*

Office politics may rear its ugly head. While you may avoid gossiping about others, you cannot prevent others from gossiping about you. Play your cards close to your chest and confide in no one. Do not mix your professional life with your private one. Tread carefully as the ground seems filled with landmines waiting for you to step on and explode. This is not an auspicious month, so avoid making careless mistakes and do not offend anyone.

This being a less than agreeable month, you should aim to lie low and maintain a low profile. Do not flaunt your talents; it will merely invite covetousness and resentment from others.

Business - *Less is more*

This month doing less is more. Do not try to interfere with the systems too much. If they are running, leave them alone. Trying to reinvent the wheel when it is working is asking for trouble. Stay out of internal politics amongst your staff. You can advise them if they come to you but avoid playing any role that involves confrontation. You don't make a good mediator now, so it is best you stay out of other people's problems. Watch the finances closely. There could be hanky panky. If people know you are looking, they will stop. Do not take large financial risks. Because you are vulnerable to loss, this could affect your business as well. An introspective period that favours planning and monitoring. It does not favour big changes, which should be left till next month when your luck is more encouraging.

Love & Relationships - *Aggressive*

You find yourself attracted to people with an aggressive nature then resent them when they try to control you. Although the Dog is naturally giving, everyone has a snapping point and this month you reach yours. If you spend too much time with those with explosive personalities, it could rub off on you. Not an agreeable time when it comes to love. If single, best to leave love matters to another time. You have a lot more to worry about than romance, and when trying to date, you could pull your problems into your budding relationship, stopping it in its tracks before you even get started.

Home & Security - *Improve security*

Protect against the loss stars that have gathered in your chart by improving home security and installing an alarm system if you have to. You can't be too careful.

Education - *Competitive*

A competitive time at school. Things are not just the way you want and you seem beset with rivals edging ahead though you have studied hard and seem in line to score. Don't let singular defeats get you down - use instead as motivation to try even harder because results will come if you keep at it.

CURE FOR THE MONTH: The Dog should carry the **Anti-Burglary Amulet** to counter the double loss stars in your chart.

10th Month
Nov 7th - Dec 6th 2021

HEAVEN STAR BRINGS RESPITE

A dramatic swing of fortune! The heavens bring new opportunities in your career and also in love. Things go magnificently, sometimes unbelievably so. You have wealth luck, so this is an opportune time to invest some of your cash in hand. Make the most of your luck by seizing opportunities that come your way. No matter how good your luck, you still need to work at it. Take the advice of older people. There is good study luck for the young Dog person. Those learning new skills find they go up the learning curve quickly. Use this time to push yourself beyond your limits. This will help launch you off any plateau you feel you have reached, taking you to exciting new heights.

Work & Career - *Be more forthcoming*

There are powerful people helping you, whether directly or behind the scenes. Being on the good side of your boss helps a lot. Work closely with your superiors. Don't let them forget you exist, because out of sight is out of mind when it comes to promotion time. If you want to make sure you're not left out, you need to be more forthcoming. While you may have the support of your boss, your peers may give you some problems. Don't pick fights; work at getting them around to your side. When you make the effort, it is difficult for anyone to resent you.

Mentors play an important role now. Don't underestimate the power of knowing the right people. This month they make all the difference.

Business - *Making deals*

Good opportunities open up as this is an excellent time for deal making. New ideas get put into motion successfully and quickly. If you are your own boss and make your own decisions then it is best, as there can be some misunderstandings between partners. Try to resolve the issues now before they get bigger. If not, agree to disagree till both sides can come to a solution. If you can come to a compromise, you can achieve a lot. Life is easier for those who can make decisions without having to check with their superiors.

Love & Relationships - *Every possibility*

A month filled with exciting possibilities in love. Also a good month to get engaged or married. If in a new relationship, now augurs well to declare your feelings. Don't worry about rejection! With heavenly luck shining down on you, only good things occur for you on the love front. More so when you are interested in the long rather than short term. For some, romance may blossom from a platonic friendship. Don't be averse to dating "your best friend". Could become the romance of the century!

Home & Family - *Celebrations*

There are excellent reasons to celebrate, so pull out all the stops, as such occasions usher in great chi and enhance your existing luck even more. You are in a position to act as mentor, either to your own child or someone's else, which will turn out to be a fulfilling experience.

Education - *Time to shine*

If you find someone who can act as mentor, you are really lucky as you stand to benefit tremendously. You have the luck to meet someone who can take you under his/her wing and who genuinely has only the best intentions. Such a role model will do you tons of good.

ENHANCER FOR THE MONTH:
Place the **Nobleman Gui Ren Talisman** on your desk, or carry one to attract beneficial mentor luck into your life.

11th Month
Dec 7th - Jan 5th 2022

FIVE YELLOW WARNS TO BE CAREFUL

The misfortune star arrives, bringing a warning to be careful. Use this month for activities that carry no risk. Relax, lie low and learn to enjoy the smaller pleasures in life. Go on holiday. Workwise, there may be some tempting offers on the table, but they come with darker undertones. If anything sounds too good to be true, it probably is. There are no free meals now. Beware getting cheated or taken for a ride. Don't owe anyone anything. Settle all your debts. You don't want to give anyone any ammunition to use against you. There is possibility of illness weakening your chi. You may be feeling out of sorts but don't let it faze you. Look on this month as a time to recharge. No harm making plans but hold off acting on them till the month is over.

Work & Career - *Avoid loose talk*

A stressful work life is not something to look forward to but this is something everyone goes through, so keep your chin up. By the end of the month you emerge stronger and more pragmatic. Avoid sharing secrets with anyone unless you wish them to be broadcast on your behalf. There is chatter going around and it is up to you whether you wish to be involved. If you retaliate by revealing juicy details, then be prepared for the positive or negative consequences. Beware what you say about others. Things you say can be misrepresented and used against you, putting you in a bad light. Better not say too much.

Business - *Avoid big moves*
Not only is your business at a low ebb, so is your mindset. You're moodier than usual and less easy to work with. Luck is not with you, so don't take chances. Stick with what you know. Avoid new ventures, new partnerships and the unknown. You want to at least have the advantage of experience and knowledge on your side. Don't sign big contracts or initiate deals now. Even if you negotiate, you end up surrendering many concessions. Obstacles crop up stalling some cherished ideas. Don't tear your hair out; things go much more smoothly next month. Wealth luck is poorly, and you need to be careful not to get played out. You can be let down even by those you trust.

Stick to what you know. Avoid venturing into unchartered territory as luck is not on your side.

Love & Relationships - *Hiccups*
You may feel you are being taken for granted or worse, taken for a ride. If so, clear the air and the sooner

the better. Throwing a tantrum or giving the silent treatment makes matters worse. Say what you feel and hear the other side out. You may have been reading the wrong signals. There are hiccups in your love life with relationships on unstable footing. Misunderstandings abound. Be prepared to apologize, forgive and forget, so you don't fall victim to the unfortunate energies of the month.

Education - *Giving up some free time*

Panic can set in if you find yourself slipping. This may set into motion a chain of events you will not be happy with, so steer yourself away from this vicious cycle. You may have to make some sacrifices if you want to do well in your studies.

CURE FOR THE MONTH: Carry the **Tree of Life Five Element Pagoda Amulet** to counter the monthly wu wang. Those in business should have the **Anti-Cheating Amulet with Kuan Kung**. This will ensure you do not get cheated by unscrupulous individuals.

12th Month
Jan 6th - Feb 3rd 2022

GOOD TIME FOR LEARNING & DISCOVERING NEW THINGS

A most favourable month for learning and discovery. Students of all kinds and those involved in research experience all kinds of epiphanies, and serious breakthroughs can be made. A productive time for anyone involved in creative work. Your oratory skills are sharpened and fine-tuned. You command attention and people are willing to listen and follow. Your powers of persuasion are now at their peak, so if up your street, you make a good spokesperson and can turn a profit just from your persuasiveness in your communications. Relationships go well for you, not just in love and romance, but in your dealings with friends, colleagues and work associates. Turn on the charm and no one can resist!

Work & Career - *Improving your skills*

Your communicative skills are at their height, but this is also a great time to improve your knowledge. You continue to learn new things on the job but if you take the extra effort to improve yourself through study, research or attending courses, the rewards come back manifold. A little investment reaps significant rewards

so do take time to consider what you can do to increase your qualifications. A month when pushing the limits lifts you to new heights.
Treat this time as a magnificent learning period as you have that kind of luck now. Do not shun new ideas or dismiss new methods of doing things.

Your colleagues are supportive and give a helping hand if asked. Accept help graciously. There are no hidden agendas and you are the main beneficiary.

Business - *Game plan*
A good time to hold important meetings, launch new products, sign deals or conduct press conferences. You are persuasive and what you say makes sense to your audience. Your ability to steer the audience, shareholders, investors or partners is unsurpassed at this time! Discussions go the way you want and being in the driver's seat has never been so productive. Strategise carefully, have a game plan, then go for it! Wealth luck is encouraging and comes from effective networking, so attend as many functions as you wish. Many end up producing sterling results. Big sales result from goodwill from those who take a personal liking to you, and from knowing the right people. The only fly in the ointment are underhand tactics from opponents. If you spot something, react quickly. Stay alert to what is going on. Don't forget that success is often accompanied by envy.

Love & Relationships - *Delicious*

A month filled with delicious encounters of a romantic nature! Love luck is powerful, making it easy to get together with anyone you may have your eye on. As good a month for the attached as well as the single Dog. If in a long-time relationship, you get the opportunity to spice things up. Even those married a long time, don't underestimate the little gestures. Making an effort now breathes new life into your marriage!

Home & Family - *Bonding*

A good time to bond with family and close friends, so seek out the company of those you haven't seen in a while. You enjoy their company and they bring fresh new ideas and perspectives.

Education - *Everyone's favourite person*

Seems like you can do no wrong! Your powers of concentration are enhanced, and everything seems stacked in your favour. A month when you can easily be everyone's favourite person - your teachers, classmates, people you meet outside of school. Others genuinely want to help you, with no ulterior motive other than to be your friend, so accept all offers.

ENHANCER FOR THE MONTH: Students and anyone wishing to learn a new skill or improve an existing one should carry the **Manjushri "Dhih" Scholastic Amulet**.